A BOOK OF UNCOMMON PRAYER

HELP ME PRAY

O Lord,
   sort out the incoherent sounds of my life.
So much of it is filled with gladness,
   and I am grateful.
I appreciate
   early morning sounds of a new day,
   high noon sounds of work in process,
   and evening sounds of relaxation and rest.

Yet much of the time
   these good sounds are overlaid with raucousness,
And my grunts of gratitude
   are drowned in loud complaints.
Give me the deep-down feeling of gladness in life
   that will keep erupting into exclamations of praise.
When I say "Thanks!" over a daily experience
   that seems good to me,
Will you hear that joyful noise
   and accept it as unto you? *Amen.*

A Book of Uncommon Prayer

Kenneth G. Phifer

THE UPPER ROOM

A Book of Uncommon Prayer
Copyright 1981, Kenneth G. Phifer

In the Upper Room printing of *A Book of Uncommon Prayer,* published in 1982, material not previously published includes "Introduction," "For the Night before Surgery," "For the Birth of a Daughter," and "For the Birth of a Son" copyright © 1982 by Kenneth G. Phifer.

Originally published by E. S. Upton Printing, New Orleans, Louisiana.

First Upper Room Printing: February 1983 (7)
Second Printing: December 1983 (5)
Third Printing: February 1986 (3)
Fourth Printing: February 1987 (3)
Book and Cover Design: Harriette Bateman
Library of Congress Catalog Card Number: 82-50945
ISBN: 0-8358-0451-8
Printed in the United States of America

CONTENTS

PRAYERS FOR UNCOMMON DAYS

INTRODUCTION

Running from God's the longest race of all.
        —Theodore Roethke

Years ago I read a newspaper account of a man wanted for murder in a midwestern state who walked into a police station to give himself up. When asked why he surrendered he answered with a shrug, "You can't run forever." You can't run forever. Yet we keep on running, most of us. Not from the police or from murder charges. We just keep on running. That is our manner of living in this latter part of the 20th century in America. We wake up in the morning running. We spend the day running. We run home at night. You are a runner if you are an average American. I am a runner. I realized it recently. Perhaps it was in part because I am getting older, and I can see that I can't run forever.

Prayer for many of us gets crowded out to the edges of life. It becomes perfunctory or detached from reality. Few of us can sit on the bank of a river to contemplate lazily and meditate in leisurely fashion. We live by the clock. How can prayer be real and vital, not just in times of crisis or in periods of withdrawal from the daily routine? How can we have a prayer life on the run? Perhaps we cannot. Perhaps we must learn the discipline of withdrawal even if the withdrawal is brief in time. Perhaps the secret is an intensity of feeling projected out from our inner selves toward God. Howard Thurman has a phrase for it. He calls it "a centering moment." He means a focusing time, a zeroing in, a pivoting instant.

Very important to such a centering moment is the readiness to begin where we are. Most of us feel we have to develop a prayerful mood. A man comes to the dinner table after a frustrating day at the office and says, "I don't feel like saying a blessing." That is understandable, and in such moments an honest recognition of a rejecting frame of mind is better than a perfunctorily muttered, routine saying of "Grace." The truest mark of prayer is the depth of feeling that generates it. That feeling may be anger or hurt, doubt or despair, exuberance or gratitude.

The prayers which follow are not structured according to any particular formula. At times they shade into meditative soliloquies. *The Directory for Worship of the Presbyterian Church* calls for "dignity and propriety" in public prayer which should embrace the following elements: adoration, thanksgiving, confession, supplication, and intercession. There is a place for such carefully organized efforts. However, the prayers which follow are not intended for public worship. They are expressions out of different moods and various situations. They are effusions of personal experiences, either mine or experiences that have become mine as I have entered into the feelings of other people. They represent times when someone quit running long enough to realize "You can't run forever," either from oneself, from other people, or from God. They are prayers for stopping places and stopping times, some brief and transitory, some longer and more contemplative.

Ruthie Frierson, an elder in the St. Charles Avenue Church and a friend, came to me in the spring of 1981 with the suggestion that certain prayers offered in public worship services be reworked and personalized and made available to members and friends of the congregation of that church. She worked diligently in the selection of the prayers and in the enlistment of the support of the Session of the church as sponsor of the project. William Bell, president of E. S. Upton Printing Co. and a deacon in the congregation, offered to publish an edition as a gift to be distributed to each family unit in the congregation with those copies left over to be sold at a minimum cost. Genevieve Munson Trimble read many prayers and made invaluable suggestions and editorial comments. My secretary, Dorothy Marchal, in addition to the labor of typing, gave indispensable aid in creating the blank verse structure of the prayers. Stanton M. (Buddy) Frazar contributed the title, and Sylvia Penn Wagner designed the cover for that edition. Anna McPheeters carefully proofread the manuscript. Without these people, this little book would not have come into being. As always, the influence of my wife, sympathetic advisor and helper, was absolutely essential.

The first printing in the fall of 1981 was distributed or sold rapidly. Bishop Edward Tullis of The United Methodist Church, an old friend of mine, brought the manuscript to the attention of Janice Grana of the Upper Room Press. I have been delighted to work with her and with Charla Honea in this second printing. With the correction of some minor typographical errors and with the addition of three prayers, the book remains as before. I have been deeply moved by its acceptance, and it goes forth now with an additional prayer that it will be helpful to some seekers and finders of the meaning of prayer in our lives.

K.G.P.

PRAYERS FOR
COMMON MOODS

I NEED REMINDING OF THE PRESENCE

Eternal God, you are love.
Your Spirit is the bright burning of hopes
   that keep me from despair.
Why do I always direct my petitions to you
   as though you were far from me?
You are near, very near.

For I have known you in the sudden shock of intimate moments,
   when I have felt a Presence not my own,
   and believed in a Comforter beyond my understanding.
You are near, very near.

For you have breathed your Spirit into me.
You have come to me in the unease I have known
   when I have wronged another and betrayed love.
You have come to me in the faith I feel in times of difficulty
   that I will somehow manage to make it through the day.
You have come to me in the glad singing
   that, at times, comes spontaneously.
You have come to me in so many ways,
   and I am grateful.
You are near, very near.

Let me be wise enough to savor and expand
   my experiences of joy and growth
      into appreciation of life's meaning.
Let me be concerned enough to try to carry to others
      my experience of the Lord Christ.
For in his Spirit
   we are called to lift, to love, to help. *Amen.*

I NEED CHILDLIKENESS

Creator and Redeemer, O God,
  you have revealed yourself,
And yet you are ever
  the great, brooding mystery beyond meaning.
I come now in my prayers
  like a little child.
Like a child,
  I am perplexed and frustrated
    when I am unable to have my own way.
Like a child,
  I pout and hide
    when I am angered.
But there, too often, the childlikeness ends.
I am too grown-up
  to be open to life's experiences joyously and freely.
I am too wise
  to believe in goodness.
I have seen too much of the world
  to be expectant and eager.
I have lived too long
  to wonder and to be amazed.
I have been hurt too often
  to be friendly with strangers.
I have learned
  to draw back from life, O Father,
  and to be guarded in manner with those I do not know.
Yet I cannot live, truly live, without these experiences.

So I come now
  like a child
  not a pouting, sulking child
    but
  like an openhearted, glad and gleeful child.
I am ready again for your Spirit. *Amen.*

I WONDER ABOUT THE MEANING OF LIFE

O God of calm and turbulence,
  of stillness and agitation:
You know me for what I am.
And I confess that that
  is more than I know of myself.
I often brood when I think
  about the meaning of my life.
I am given to wondering moodily
  upon its frustrations and contradictions.
Sometimes I do think about who I am
  and why I am here.
But not for long.

For the most part, I just take life as it comes.
Some of it is good,
  some is bad.
Some of it is fulfilling,
  some disappointing.
I win a little,
  lose a little.
I laugh a little,
  cry a little.
I try to avoid too much involvement
  for I know I can be hurt,
And I know other people are being hurt needlessly.
I know there are greed and corruption,
  and I am disturbed a little—
    but only temporarily.
But what can I do, Lord?
I have to live with the world as it is, don't I?

Or do I?
Am I really called upon
  to be a world changer?
Do you really expect me
  to count for something,
  to be a bit like Jesus?
Must I be lover and helper,
  lifter and healer?

Lord, I am not sure
  I can be who and what you call me to be in Christ.

Is that because I lack faith,
  or is it lack of desire?
Fitting in is so much easier
  than reaching out.
Taking the world as it is is so much more comfortable
  than taking Jesus seriously.
Hedging my bets is so much safer
  than gambling my reputation.
Yet I go to church and pray
  and find it all makes me uneasy.
I really do want to be more Christian,
  in my heart and in my life.
Help me to go about it,
  and go with me, I pray, for Jesus' sake. *Amen*

I NEED TO BE OPEN TO YOU

Lord God,
   you are beyond my comprehension and understanding,
Yet you seem very near.
Something within me makes me reach out,
   makes me want to pray.
I want to feel that I am in touch with something
   or someone beyond myself.
I want to lean upon a rock,
   steadier than my wobbling spirit and my erratic will.
I need a strength greater than my own,
   a power that is more than the power I can generate.
I boast at times.
I strut about importantly.

Yet I know I am easily frightened
   by events over which I have no control,
So I bluster and shout.
I am secretly unsure that I can manage my life,
So I defiantly express my own dogmatic and differing opinions.
I am terribly confused
   by a world that makes little sense at times.
So I insist I have all the answers,
If only other people would stop talking and listen to me.

Lord, I cannot ask to be made fearless
   in such a world as ours,
For only a fool could be unafraid.
I cannot ask to be made absolutely certain
   of how things should go,
For no human can assume infallibility.
I cannot even ask to be exempt from perplexity,
For life is marked by the process of trial and error.
I cannot expect deliverance from pressure and tension,
   from conflicts engendered by human differences,
   from problems created by our own blundering.
What can I ask?

Steadiness—
   to hang on to hope in spite of my fears.

Openness—
    to listen to other voices from other rooms,
      in spite of their strangeness.
Commitment—
    to those things in which I believe,
    to affirm them in the face of opposition.
I can ask for those things, O God,
    for I know I badly need them.
And I know you have promised them
    in Jesus Christ our Lord. *Amen.*

I FEEL BORED

I am weary.
There is so little lift to my daily experiences,
   so little romance.
I never seem to meet the unexpected.
My life is so organized and structured
   that I would like, at times,
     to flee to far-away places with strange-sounding names.
I know now exactly what I will do in the week ahead.
I am bored.
I am fed up with my job,
   sick of the tedium of my day-to-day responsibilities.
I would like, O Lord,
   to feel that I really matter
   and that my small efforts count for something.

How can I know life adds up?
Can I discover some of the meaning of it now
   through my prayers?
I do not expect to hear a voice speaking to me,
   but I would like to feel your Presence.
I do not ask for any handwriting on the walls,
   but I would like to feel an upsurge of faith.
If I cannot wholly commit myself
   to belief in your concern for me,
Give me, at least, a nudge in that direction.
I believe in you,
   God the Father Almighty,
   Maker of Heaven and Earth,
     and of me too.
You are my Creator and,
   if we are to believe our Lord Jesus,
You are my Redeemer.
Does that mean you work in me
   to eliminate the anxious self-centeredness
     that keeps me from abundant living?
Does that mean that you save me,
   not just from the big booming sins of wild abandon
     that few of us are given to,

But from the little nasty sins of which I am ashamed?
If this is what redemption means,
    I want it.
Give me courage to accept it,
    and the faith to live a life redeemed from boredom,
In the Spirit of Christ. *Amen.*

I AM IMPATIENT

O Lord our God,
When I stop to think upon life,
   I am amazed by its diversity.

There is a time—
   to give thanks for the sheer rapture of living,
   to ask for help in the bearing of burdens,
   to ask for surcease from pain.

There is a time—
   to cry out,
   to be still,
   to seize the opportunity that lies at hand,
     to wait until the night has gone,
       and the dawn has come once more,
         and hope trembles naked in the chill of morning.

There is a time—
   to pray,
   to refrain from praying,

Simply waiting in the silence for a sound of music
   that will set our spirits to dancing again.

I confess, O Lord, my problem lies in my inability
   to unravel the complexity of my own experiences.

I take life's rapturous moments for granted,
   only to look back and see that I gave no thanks.

I struggle on blindly through my days of difficulty,
   realizing too late that I have asked for no help either from you
     or from those who love me and would like to help.

I have tried to go it alone.

I have stormed heaven with my strident demands
   when there was no need.

You are my Father and, like a good father,

you are sensitive to my needs,
concerned about my predicaments.

Help me to remember that you are standing by,
offering me the courage and faith necessary
to see me through another day and another night.

So I can rein my impatience and wait.

At least I think I can, with your help
and with the example of our Lord Jesus Christ. *Amen*

I FEEL IRRITABLE

At times, I confess,
   I am not very thankful to be part of this world.
I would like to get off.
I would like to escape.
Yet I keep coming back
     to the basic goodness of your creation,
  rediscovering mirth and music,
     love and kindness,
     acceptance and hope.
I keep quarreling with those aspects of life
     that distort goodness.
I quarrel with pain.
I quarrel with injustice.
I quarrel with brutality.
Keep me quarreling, Father,
     with the world as it is,
But deliver me from becoming simply querulous and cross,
     judgmental and hateful,
Thus adding to the distortion
     and contributing to the twisting of life
     from the beautiful to the grotesque.
May my quarrel with the world be a lover's quarrel.
May my anger be the anger of one
  who knows his own part
    in the marring of your world's beauty
  and is repentant.

Let this recognition not depress me but alert me,
    not lead me to despise myself but to accept forgiveness.
Let the knowledge that others have marred life, too,
    not lead me to despise them but to be forgiving.
For we all fail to love enough,
   to care enough,
   to involve ourselves enough.

So I come back to you, O Lord, for help.
I need it.
I have to go on.

Keep me on the right track
   as far as you are able,
For I am stubborn and self-willed often,
   and, occasionally, sobered and humbled. *Amen.*

I FEEL DISCOURAGED

O Lord God, you have created me,
And in that creation,
  you have placed within me the image of yourself.
I know not what that means
  except I have longings and aspirations
    not satisfied by the things of earth.
I reach.
I wonder.
I want.
I pray.
I have intimations of immortality and glimpses of heaven.
I hope.
I dream.
I love.
I am not always brave
  but I exalt courage.
I am not always honest
  but I respect truth.
I am not always loving
  but I would like to be.

O Lord, deliver me from discouragement
    over the way the world goes.
    over the way I go.
keep me from losing faith
    when things go badly,
    when values seem lost.
In a time when virtues seem irrelevant,
  let me not assume
    there are no standards of goodness and truth.

For I know that because you are.
  there is hope.
Because you are,
  there is truth.
Because you are,
  I am.
Hold on to me, O Lord,
    when I cannot hold on to you. *Amen.*

I NEED A MIRACLE

You who have been my dwelling place.
    whom I have not always known,
    whom I have not always acknowledged,
  yet who has sustained me and kept me,
Hear me as I pray.
Hear me and make me know that you are,
    that I live in you.
I try so hard to live apart from you.
I boast of my own sufficiency.
I proudly assert my independence.
I proclaim my ability
    to handle myself,
    to handle my world.
I whistle loudly in the dark
    to cover the pounding of my frightened heart.
For I am not self-sufficient,
    not really independent.
I handle things rather badly.
I cannot handle my anxieties and my anger,
    my prejudices, loneliness, and death.
I want some help,
And in the solitude I cast off my pride.
Will you come to me in the deep places of my spirit?

I do not want epiphanies
    of flame and thunder,
    of voices and apparitions in the night.
Such things would only frighten me.
I do want a sense of belonging in the universe,
    of being loved,
    of being able to love others,
    of acceptance,
    of being able to accept others.
I want warmth in relationships,
    joy in the good things of earth,
    and a faith that whatever tomorrow brings,
      I won't be alone.

I want to be fully human,
   unafraid of myself,
   and unthreatened by other people.
If I could have these things,
   they would be miracle enough. *Amen.*

I DO NOT KNOW WHAT TO DO

Eternal God,
   I stammer at my prayers,
   I falter when I call your name.
I confess I too often say what I feel I ought to say,
     using words learned long ago in childhood
     and phrases memorized once without commitment.
I am carefully selective
   as though I could disguise my true feelings from you.
Forgive me that I do not trust you more,
   that I so often feel I must maintain
     a facade between myself and you.
Hear me now as I pray
   in the silent places of my heart.

I am concerned about my feelings, O Lord;
   I am not sure what they really are.
I find myself torn by inner conflicts,
     tense with divided loyalties.
I know you have called me
     to love of my brothers and concern for my neighbors,
But love and concern are hard to come by.
I live in a world marked with hatred
     and stamped with suspicion.
I am afraid of many of my neighbors,
     and rightly so.
I live in a world of force and violence.
I am afraid of appearing puny.
I call Jesus "Lord,"
   but sometimes I secretly suspect that his way is futile.
I want to be sort of like him
     but not too much.
How can I be expected to bear crosses,
     to turn other cheeks?
You know who I am, O Lord.
What will people think of me
     unless I talk tough and loud?

Deep down within me, O Lord,
     is the need for your guidance.

I will face situations this week
    when I will not know what to do.
I will be in circumstances
    where I will not know what to say.
I will read of events in the world around me
    and I will not know how to think.
Keep me from the hasty action,
        the careless word,
        the unthought-out reaction.
Steady me that I may know
    your Spirit has not been withdrawn from my world,
    and your Presence is still with me.
"Be thou my Guide." *Amen.*

I WANT TO BE LESS SELF-ABSORBED

I know, O Lord,
    that it is only when I am honest about myself
    that I can pray for others.
I do want to move beyond my self-absorption
    to greater awareness of those around me.
Free me to do that,
    to think upon those
      who have just cause to resent me.
    to ask forgiveness for the wrong things
      I have done to others;
Not just the great big acts of betrayal,
    but the little ways in which I have hurt someone
      by deprecating words
      or chilly silence
      or petty accusations.
Loosen me to feel my oneness with others
      from whom I hold aloof:
    the unpleasant people whom I simply do not like,
    the people whom I do not know
      and do not want to know
    because of their race or religion or economic status.
Free me and loosen me, O Lord God,
    to be more like our Lord Jesus. *Amen.*

I NEED MORE FAITH

Give me, O Lord, a greater faith.
Teach me what faith is about.
I so often confuse faith
    with a long list of things to believe.
I so often get faith mixed up
    with creeds recited and words said.
Teach me how the creeds recited and the words said
    are only our feeble, fumbling human ways
        of trying to affirm that which takes place
        in the human spirit when,
            in trust and faith,
            that spirit turns toward you.

Turn me, O God.
Turn my heart upward
    out of the valley of fear wherein sometimes I walk.
Turn my spirit sunward
    out of the dim despair amid which sometimes I grope.
Turn my feelings on,
    that I may not be afraid of accepting the goodness of life,
    a goodness that shines and shines
        even through the gloom of adverse circumstances.

Let me not be afraid to love this world,
        its beauty and wonder,
        its things of the flesh,
        and its things of the spirit.
Give me appreciation for the things
    I can handle and touch.
Give me appreciation for the people I know.
It is so easy to pass people by,
        to look over the heads of others,
        to look past the hurt, the needy, the lonely.
Let me not be afraid.
Lift me out of my anxieties
        into the kind of confidence
    that will give me strength and courage.
Deliver me from turning away from life.

Keep me from being overwhelmed
      by the pains, the tensions, the angers
           of a world like mine.
How can I be overwhelmed if you are God
     and if your Spirit is at work?
How can I turn away
     if that Man of Galilee is still beckoning to me
          to join him in his work of redemption and reconciliation?

Let me, O God,
     keep faith with the best I know and feel.
Let me act out of my own integrity
     and remain loyal to my highest ideals.
I am not always sure I am right.
But then, you have a marvelous way of using people
     who can admit they are not always right;
     people who keep seeking new insights and new visions.
It comforts us wobblers to know
     that you seem to have the most trouble
          with people who are most sure
     they have a monopoly on truth and virtue.
I have a hard time being humble enough to be teachable.
I know, O Lord,
     you will do the best you can with me day by day,
And I also know that if I will let you,
     you will do more with me tomorrow
          than I let you do yesterday.

Keep my face toward the future
     with confidence in you
     as your Spirit works within me.
Through Jesus Christ our Lord. *Amen.*

I AM NOT SURE HOW TO PRAY

How should I pray, O Lord?
Should I wait until my life is cleansed
    and my spirit is hot?
Or should I come just as I am
        with my half-hearted commitment
        and my on-again, off-again faith?
How should I pray?

Should I choose my words carefully
    and phrase my petitions with discrimination?
Should I sit very straight and very still?
Or should I let my needs roll out
    and my doubts and difficulties show?
How should I pray,
    O God of the morning sun and the evening shadow?
How should I pray in the high, hot noon of life?
I really do not know.

Once our Lord told us we should pray like this:
    "Our Father, who art in heaven,
    Hallowed be Thy name...."
And then he poured out petitions
    about daily bread and forgiveness of others
        that we may be forgiven...
    temptations to be delivered from...
    evil to be spared.
Those are all things that press in upon us all.

So I do pray for daily bread.
I pray for the material things of life
        that I may have what I can use,
        and that I may use what I have.
I pray for the grace
        to exercise forgiveness where I have been wronged.
Deliver me from the stuffy, condescending attitude
    of self-righteousness.
Help me to have the honesty and the courage
        to accept my share of responsibility
            where broken relationships obtain.

Keep me from simply using words
　　to cover a rejecting spirit.

I ask to be delivered from temptations
　　and to be delivered from deceiving myself
　　　　about my temptations.
For, too often, I only mean that
　　I want to be rescued
　　　　from the consequences of my behavior.
And the evil from which I desire to be spared is,
　　too often,
　　the result of my headlong pursuit of my selfish whims.
I try to put burdens on you, O God,
　　that are mine to bear.
I try to avoid the strain on my own will power,
　　and call upon my sense of love
　　　　by asking you to take responsibility.
I know I should not,
　　and yet I do.

How should I pray, O God?
I do not really know how I should,
　　but I have prayed as best I can.
And where I have left unsaid
　　what should have been said,
　　O Lord of the heart,
Take the intention for the deed. *Amen.*

I FIND IT HARD TO BELIEVE

Eternal God,
   it is hard to believe
     that you want what I have to give,
     that you take me as I am,
      where I am.
I find it difficult to trust you,
   else I would not be so uptight and tense,
    so anxious and uncomfortable.
Yet the Lord Jesus taught us to come to you
    in the naturalness of our undressed lives,
    and in the disorder of our chaotic spirits.
So I come.
I cannot wear white garments of innocence
   for I have spotted my life
    with all sorts of unworthy things
     of which I am ashamed.
Still, I know you do not want me berating myself,
   and lamenting my wickedness.
You want me to rise into the clear light
   of your acceptance and forgiveness.
I cannot come in serene complaisance.
I am troubled in various ways.
I have insoluble problems,
   unresolved difficulties in relationships.
I know you do not want me to wait
   until I am in control of my life.
You want me to open myself to your Spirit
    with the knowledge that,
    if my problems remain insoluble,
   I can live with them by your grace.
So I come.

I come, O Lord,
   moving in the right direction, I hope.
I come, O Lord,
   turned toward the light that you offer.
And if in my coming, my moving, my turning,
   I am strengthened,

That is enough.
It is more than I can manage alone.

But then, there is little I can manage alone.
I need other people,
    and above all,
I need you, O God. *Amen.*

I WANT TO STOP RUNNING

Eternal God, you are a song amid silence,
   a voice out of quietness,
   a light out of darkness,
   a Presence in the emptiness,
   a coming out of the void.
You are all of these things and more.
You are mystery that encompasses meaning,
   meaning that penetrates mystery.
You are God,
   I am man.
I strut and brag.
I put down my fellows
   and bluster out assertions of my achievements.
And then something happens:
   I wonder who I am,
     and if I matter.
Night falls,
   I am alone in the dark and afraid.
Someone dies,
   I feel so powerless.
A child is born,
   I am touched by the miracle of new life.
At such moments I pause ...
   to listen for a song amid silence,
   a voice out of stillness,
   to look for a light out of darkness.
I want to feel a Presence in the emptiness.
I find myself reaching for a hand.

Oftentimes, the feeling passes quickly,
   and I am on the run again:
     success to achieve,
     money to make.
O Lord, you have to catch me on the run most of the time.
I am too busy to stop,
   too important to pause for contemplation.
I hold up too big a section of the sky
     to sit down and meditate.
But even on the run,

an occasional flicker of doubt assails me,
And I suspect I may not be as important to the world
   as I think I am.
Jesus said each of us is important to you.
It is as if every hair of our heads were numbered.
How can that be?
But in the hope that it is so,
I would stop running,
     stop shouting,
   and be myself.

Let me be still now.
Let me be calm.
Let me rest upon the faith that you are, God,
   and I need not be afraid. *Amen.*

I NEED TO FEEL WHOLE

O God, what is Spirit?
How do I worship in spirit and in truth?
I am such a solid, earthly creature,
    my feet planted firmly on the ground,
    my life based upon material things.
I like to touch and feel and see before I believe.
I am accustomed to dealing with houses, land, and money,
    with bread, meat, and potatoes,
    with objects handled, weighed, and valued
        by my own standards.
I am uncomfortable with what cannot be analyzed or dissected
    or given a market value.
What is Spirit?

Yet, O Lord, the very things I handle and see
    lose meaning when they become ends in themselves.
They are all given meaning by the things of the spirit,
    by love and hope and faith.
I know when I come down to it,
  if I have all kinds of earthly goods
    and have not love,
  I have nothing.
I need the mystery beyond the tangible.
I need the things of the spirit
  to give meaning to the material things I prize.
I cannot divide life up,
  you have made it whole.
If I avoid love, diminish hope, deny faith,
  my appreciation of my house and land,
  my meat and potatoes, shrinks,
And I become a little man
  with little aims and little power.

So help me to see that I worship in spirit and in truth,
  not just through the use of the right words
    in the right place at the right time.
I worship in spirit and in truth
    as life assumes wholeness.

I worship in spirit
    as life takes on shape and form,
  and I glory in it all.
I worship in truth insofar as I know that
  no life can be separated from your Spirit.
I worship as I offer it all unto you. *Amen.*

I NEED TO EXPAND MY FAITH

I believe, O God, I believe.
I am not always sure what I believe
    or how to express what I believe,
But I believe.

I believe, at times only in fuzzy ways,
        that somehow, somewhere,
        good is real and love matters.
But then at times I believe
        in vibrant, exciting, concrete experiences
            of your grace.
I feel that the Lord Jesus Christ is real
    and the Holy Spirit is present in my world
        and in my life.
I believe in joyous ways
        that life is worthwhile,
    and that I matter to you and to other people.
I am grateful for such experiences of believing.

Sometimes I feel myself cast down and despairing,
        incapable of trust and skeptical of hope.
And from the midst of my desolation,
    I am pushed back into life and relationships again.
I know I have gone on,
        not in my own strength,
            but in a strength from beyond,
    and with surprise I know that you have done the pushing.
I believe, O Lord.

I've known times of regret,
    hours when my memory has blushed with shame
        and my spirit has been lashed with guilt.
I have been sorry for deeds that could not be undone
        and for words that could not be taken back.
I have repented,
        and in my sense of inner disgrace,
    there has suddenly come a healing and a hope.
I believe, O God, in forgiveness.

I ask forgiveness now that so much of the time is spent
  fruitlessly churning along in life
    outside the power of my beliefs.
If I truly believe life is worthwhile,
  why am I so bored?
If I know that you never leave us alone in our estrangement,
  why do I feel so deserted?
And if I believe in forgiveness,
  why do I not accept it and live in the joy of salvation?

I believe, O God, that you have a place for me,
  that I am part of your plan.
I believe,
  but too often my belief is so small.
Give me the courage to believe big,
    to love big,
      and to hope big for myself and others.
I believe.
Help my unbelief through Jesus Christ our Lord. *Amen.*

I NEED TO BE REMINDED OF GOD'S CARE

Eternal God,
Lord of all life,
I, your forgetful child, now remind myself
    of my final dependence upon your grace.
So often in my prayers I use phrases like
  "Remember me, O God,"
  "Hear me now, O Lord,"
  "Look with favor upon me."
How foolish such phrases are!
You remember me in the midst of my forgetting.
You hear me when I make the tiniest squeak.
You look with favor upon me when I cannot stand myself.
But things are the other way round.
I am the one who needs to be reminded
    that you do not turn from me,
  I turn from you.
You do not forget me,
  I forget you.
You do not despise me even when I err and go astray,
  I despise myself.

Old brown yesterdays haunt and trouble me.
Old wounds ache, and old bruises give me pain.
Let me recall old promises.
For you have said,
  "Ho, everyone who is thirsty, come to the waters,
  and he who has no money, come, buy and eat."
I am parched and dry, O Lord.
I am hungry for affirmations in life.
I come, tentatively,
  just hoping and not really believing.
But I come. *Amen.*

I WONDER WHO I AM

O Lord my God,
I am called to prayer so many times
    and in so many ways.
Over and over,
  my spirit turns to prayer instinctively.
The sun rises, the sun sets.
The rain falls.
The wind sings in the night.
The stars shine.
  And my heart says, "Thank you."
I am caught by surprising moments of unexpected joy.
  I laugh, I cry.
  I catch my breath in sheer delight.
  My soul chuckles, "Thank you, whoever you are."

Pain-filled hours haunt me.
  I weep, I moan.
  Sometimes I want to die.
Yet even then,
    or especially then,
  I ask, "Help me, if you are."

Who am I, O Lord?
Why am I here?
Am I deceived when I feel I matter,
    that I count,
    that someone cares?
I give you a name—"Father"
  and I think of a face and features
    like those of Jesus Christ.
Then I go my way, grateful and praying.

I am called to prayer.
I believe,
    in the rising and setting sun,
    in the wind and the stars.
But what is far more important,
  I believe in life, my life.

I confess that, at times,
  my faith is unsure,
  my trust is tentative,
  my love is cautious.
But you keep surrounding me with evidences of amazing grace,
  and I take heart once more.
I can make it,
  not in my own power,
    but in yours. *Amen.*

I FEEL DISSATISFIED

Eternal God,
Fashioner of dreams,
I pray that you will touch
    that which is within me to flame.
I know not what lies deep within my spirit.
I only know that I am restless at times,
    dissatisfied upon occasion,
  feeling there is more to life than I have known.
I feel there is love I have not explored,
    faith I have not dared,
    music I have not heard.
I am bound-in, uptight, circumscribed,
    and smaller than I feel I might be.
Loosen me from the anxieties that hem me in.
Free me from the fears that hold me back.

Loosen me, O God,
  that I may trust what I profess to know of you.
I call you the God of Grace
  and then live in such ungainly fashion.
I am awkward in my relationships to others,
    with sharp edges of anger
    and jagged points of abrasiveness.
I want to reach out in helpfulness,
  and I am tied in knots by feelings of inadequacy.
Free me to be more open,
    both in giving and receiving.
I am even self-conscious in prayer,
    fearful of revealing myself to you
  as though you did not know me better
    than I know myself.
I conceal my real feelings,
  deny my doubts,
    and smooth out my complaints.
Free me and loosen me, O Lord God,
    to be more like our Lord Jesus.

For it is he whom I would serve,
    and it is he whose words come to me
        as words about life.
Touch that tiny spark within me
    and fan it to a blaze.
I ask this in Jesus' name. *Amen.*

I NEED TO BE MORE LOVING

Almighty God,
I know so little of what love in its fullness can be.
My love is marred by jealousy,
    scarred by envy,
        limited by selfishness.
I withhold love at the slightest provocation,
    and withdraw myself from involvement with others
        for fear of being hurt.

Still, I know something of what love can be like.
I can remember being forgiven generously and freely
    by someone I had wronged.
I can remember being comforted and cared for
    when, bruised and battered, I crept home.
I can remember being made strong
    by the realization that someone cared.
I am grateful for such experiences,
    for they tell me what love is about.
And if the Lord Jesus be right,
    to know what love is like
    is to know what you are like.

If we humans can manifest unselfishness and concern,
    is it not because such experiences are of the very nature
        of that which is most important?
For out of the heart of the Lord Jesus
    came the evidences of his love
        for all kinds of people
    and his refusal to give up on any of us.
I am grateful for that love and for that refusal,
    for in him I have hope.
I can even hope
    that I may catch more of his Spirit in my life.

Will you help me to be more outgoing,
    less sensitive to slights,
        and more alert to the feelings of others?
Will you help me to be less quick to judge
    and less righteous in my indignation?

Will you help me to be more open to life
and to other people?
Will you give me confidence enough to be less defensive
and less ready to react to rebuffs?
Give me steadiness and firmness
and true commitment to the life of faith. *Amen.*

I NEED RENEWAL

O Lord our God,
You have given me the gift of life,
  and when I abuse it you restore me
    that I may try again.
You are both a conservationist and a restorationist.
You work within me to conserve that which I never quite lose,
  the sense of the holiness of life
    that I never quite obliterate,
  the reverence I feel at least occasionally,
  and the wonder I know now and again.
Your Spirit works within
    to deepen and broaden my appreciation
      for the gift of life,
  and I am grateful.
When left to myself,
  I confess I grow careless and blunder along,
    bumping into other people and jostling them aside,
    stomping on flowers and tromping across the grass.
I forget to pray and neglect praise.
But you keep working within me,
    making me restless in my boorishness
    and discontented with my clumsy handling of life.
Deliver me from ever settling down,
    satisfied in rude rejection of love and faith and hope.

Restore me, I pray, for I need restoration.
I do not ask to be put back into the shape I once was.
I know that the very experiences that have marred me,
    even scarred me,
    and have given my life its weatherbeaten quality,
  are the experiences by which I have grown and learned.
I pray that I may be refurbished within,
    that my mind may be refurnished,
    and my heart redecorated
      with joy and gladness. *Amen.*

I AM TEMPTED TO HATE

Eternal God,
I can identify hatred by its mean little eyes
    and its clinched fists.
  Make me big enough to love, love, love.
I know injury when I have suffered it.
  Help me to be magnanimous as our Lord Jesus was.
I know about doubt.
I have felt it threaten to shake my security to pieces.
  Give me the kind of faith
    that hangs on and hangs in there.
Deliver me from incapacitating despair;
  wander with me
    in whatever my particular kind of darkness may be.
And when I am sad,
  let not my sadness so overwhelm me
    that I forget the rumble of joy
      at the heart of the universe.
I know I ask a lot, O God,
  when I ask for these gifts of the Spirit.

So I rest back for these moments of prayer
  on my faith that you are.
I breathe deeply and relax the tense will,
    the rigid self-control,
    the taut fixed features
  of the image I maintain before my fellow human beings.
I just am who I am with you,
  O God of Life.

Make me an instrument of your peace,
  so that where there is hatred, I can love,
  where there is injury, I can pardon.
In the spirit of him
  who was the great instrument of your salvation,
    even Jesus Christ our Lord. *Amen.*

IT'S MORNING AGAIN

I need to pray
   and I know I need to pray.
Yet I often wonder if I know how to pray.
I will be quiet for a moment.
Perhaps that is as close as I can come to prayer,
      or perhaps in my quietness,
   I will feel a Spirit not my own.
Eternal God, I am still and I am waiting.
Touch me
   where raw places of anger and hurt are to be found.
Heal me
   where open wounds of disappointment and pain gape.
Restore me
   where I need restoration.
And reconcile me
   where I am separated from you and from others.

How great you are, O God.
You can draw beauty out of barrenness,
      courage out of fear,
      and love out of loneliness.
You can make darkness as light
      and silence into singing.
You can help me handle my troubles
   or learn to live with them
      when they cannot be handled.
You can make each day a miracle of grace
   and fill each night with music.

You understand even my failures to respond to life
      as our Lord Jesus did.
You keep pressing in upon me with your forgiveness
   and offering me new chances.
Give me the courage
      to accept the chances that are mine this day.

Stir me to a new eagerness for life
and a new openness to love.
Deepen my ability to appreciate ordinary gifts
and extraordinary evidences of grace.
Sweep me clean of the petty harassments
that so often set the tone for my daily living. *Amen.*

I CANNOT ESCAPE

Eternal God, where shall I go from your Spirit?
Where shall I flee from your Presence?
For you are the grace of life,
    the constant presence of faith and hope and love.
If I ascend into the highest experience of beauty and love,
  you are there.
If I descend into the squalor of the hells of my own making,
  behold, you are there seeking me out,
    to draw me back into the sunlight of your love.
There are no experiences
    that are outside the realm of your grace.
There are no places in life
    that are bereft of your Presence.
I need reminding of that, O God,
  for I sometimes feel that I am alone,
    that I must make it on my own.
And I must confess, O Lord,
  that at times I want to feel
    that I have escaped from your Presence.
I indulge myself.
I satiate myself.
I plunge into life on my own terms
    without thought for you or for others.
I had rather be left alone.
For to feel you near reminds me
    that selfishness is not the end
    for which I am created.
I had rather be left alone.
For if I think of the Lord Jesus Christ,
  I am reminded of love and generosity,
    of self-giving and concern for others.
But I am not able to avoid those occasional pricks of conscience
    and those occasional qualms that make me a bit ashamed.

Is it true, O God,
  that I cannot go far enough
    to leave your Spirit behind?
That I cannot flee from your Presence?

Is it true that I am created to pray and give thanks,
to seek fulfillment in a spirit
that is beyond me ?

Even the darkness of pain and loss
hides not from you, O Lord.
For you are near.
Open my mind and heart and life
to your continuing Presence.
So as I look about the world
with its needy people and its perplexing problems,
let me look with eyes of faith and hope and love.
You are here, there, and everywhere.
Let me not forget.
Through Jesus Christ our Lord. *Amen*

I NEED TO BE AWARE

Expand my awareness, O God,
    to others whom I shall see today, tomorrow.
Help me to look for signs
    of our common humanity among the people I meet.
Help me to listen to what people are saying to me,
    not just to their words
  but to what they are really saying.
Sensitize me to calls for help that I might give.
Alert me to signals that I can heed if I will.

In this big, booming world of ours,
I am always bumping into people,
    then glancing off to pursue my restless, lonely ways.
I need to constantly remind myself
        that life and love are found in relationships,
        that you are speaking to me through human voices
        and touching me by means of human hands.

I pray for others and thereby touch them with my thoughts —
    ill people who know what it is to hurt and to be afraid,
    lonely people who know what it is to hunger
        for someone's concern,
    pressured people who fear they are going to crack.
As I think upon those whom I know
        and touch them with my thoughts,
    help me to whatever extent I can touch them with my life.
As I feel my way along in prayers,
    so may I feel my way along in my daily relationships,
        looking, listening, reaching out, touching.
As I would keep alive the memory of Jesus,
    give me a fuller measure of his living and healing Spirit. *Amen.*

I NEED A NEW DIRECTION

Quietly, contemplatively, I would come to prayer,
  O Lord God,
Seeking a steadying, a refocusing, and a reshaping of my life.
So much of my existence is spent
      in scrambling, searching, even clawing my way
          along the roads I walk,
      that I forget what quietness and contemplation are.
I even forget who you are
  and how you are revealed in the Man from Galilee.
He too knew his moments of scrambling,
      his hours of searching.
But somehow he manifested the steadiness
      that kept him from ever abandoning
          his commitment to life,
  no matter what the pressure.
I would be like him if I could.
But since I cannot,
  will you make me the best I can be?
Will you give me more faith and less cockiness,
      more assurance and less bravado,
      more serenity and less boastfulness?
I have my secret fears and my hidden insecurities.
I cloak them from my friends
      and deny them to my loved ones.
Yet you know them,
  and it is a relief to know that I cannot hide from you.
I would be honest now and confess my needs.
I have been ashamed of myself
      more often than I like to remember.
I have acted shabbily and harbored slovenly purposes.
I have excused myself to others and to myself.
Now I cannot cover up who I am, for I am at prayer.
I know I can make no demands but I can offer myself as I am
      with the hope that in the power of your Spirit,
  I can become more trustworthy and more dependable.
If I can, by your grace,
      be refocused and reshaped in faith and love,
      then I will be more like him and most myself. *Amen.*

I FEEL UNINVOLVED

Almighty God, who has called and called
  and whom I seldom hear,
Let my heart be open now and my spirit alert to your voice.
I know you understand
    that it is not always out of sheer indifference
      that I do not hear.
Your voice is still and small,
    as a long-ago prophet said,
  and the other voices are so loud and demanding.
You never speak in thunder.
Your comings are not marked by the roll of drums
    or the blast of trumpets.
I wish you would speak louder.
I wish your advents were plainer.
But you persist in speaking in quiet ways
    and coming in a fashion
  that makes it easy for me to ignore you.
Our Lord Jesus spoke of the naked and the hungry,
    the homeless and the imprisoned,
    the sick and the strangers,
And he warned us our response to such people
    would be the tests of our awareness of him.
But is that fair, O Lord?
I spend much of my time avoiding such people.
I do not even want to think about them.
Certainly, I do not want to be involved.
Can you not come to me some oher way?

Gropingly, I reach out in prayer now for others —
    for men and women who bear burdens of responsibility
      in a tragedy-ridden world,
    for those who stand in places of trust
      in church and state.
Gropingly, I pray for those who differ from me
    politically and ecclesiastically.
If I am not enthusiastic in such prayers,
  it is because I am threatened by differences.

Help me to be more secure
   so that I will not be thrown off balance
      by the failure of others
   to see the infallibility of my opinions.

I do sometimes reach out toward others.
When I touch another life and feel response,
   I am startled and thrilled.
Why do I keep my hands in my pockets so much of the time?
It must be that it all comes back to my failure
      to hear your still, small voice.
Those other voices of fear and hate are so loud.

Now I am listening.
Say something, O God, to me.
I am waiting. *Amen.*

I NEED TO ASSESS WHAT IS IMPORTANT

O, God of all mercies,
Lord of compassion and grace,
I live and move and have my being
    in a world which you have made.
I walk under your blue heavens
    and touch your good earth.
I look with gladness
    upon those splotches of color we call flowers
  and feel the probing fingers of the rain that makes them grow.
I behold sunrises and sunsets,
    hear birds sing,
    and smell jasmine blossoms on the night air.
My senses come alive, and I know I am of earth, earthy.
You have made me to see and feel
    and touch and enjoy life.

But I get away from those elemental relationships.
I walk on concrete pavement and drive past beauty.
The sounds of traffic and sirens drown out bird songs.
The jasmine is smothered by the pollution of the atmosphere.
I become jaded and harassed, impatient and hurried.
City buildings block my view of dawns and dusks.
I know we cannot tear up pavements and fling down buildings.
I am not going to give up my automobile.
    or shut off the air-conditioning.
I am grateful for so many of the products of human technology
    that make life more pleasant
    and alleviate so much of its drudgery.
But I am aware that while I have gained much,
  I have given up much.

Can I, O Lord, learn how to use my possessions
    and be less used by them?
Can I recapture some sense of the beauty of your creation
    and be less enamored of my creations?
You made the rivers and streams,
    the mountains and trees.
We have made factories and houses,
    plants and barns.

I am not guilty of evil for these creations of ours,
But I must confess that I have often forgotten
    that the earth is yours and all the goodness thereof.
And in my eagerness to build more barns
    and to possess more things,
I have badly managed that part of the creation
  you have entrusted to me.

Lord, I keep rationalizing my acquisitiveness.
I even do it in my relations with my neighbors.
I remain on the defensive much of the time
    lest someone take advantage of me or violate my rights.
I suppose some defensiveness is necessary to survive,
But, O God, when I am honest,
    I must admit I overdo it.
Would more openness to others destroy me?
Would kindness weaken me?
Would generosity deplete me,
    or do I just like to think so?
For, it is true, openness exposes me to hurt,
    my kindness may be treated with contempt,
    and generosity may cause me to sacrifice something.
But then, in your Presence
    and in the presence of the Cross of Jesus,
    I know that you have not spared yourself.

I wonder if fulfillment can come to me
    when I am all scrunched up in self,
    all boundaried and bordered and fenced in by self.
If I do wonder a bit now in your Presence
    and before the Cross,
    don't let me get away unchanged.
Touch me and change me,
    and if I have been converted before,
Convert me again.
    I need it. *Amen.*

I NEED HELP WITH MY PROBLEMS

O Lord our God,
  I have problems that I must am not handling too well.
I have difficulties in understanding other people.
I have secret angers and not so secret resentments
    that leave me irritable.
I have anxieties about the future
    and regrets concerning the past
  that I cannot put aside.
Will you help me at these places, O God?

Give me the insight to realize
  that I do not have to hide behind artificial feelings.
I can even come to you wth honest doubts and nagging fears.
For is it not because of my doubts that I try to pretend?
  I do not really believe that you accept me as I am.
Is it not because of my fears
    that I attempt to disguise my feelings?
I do not have faith in your ability
    to understand my humanness.

My needs, I know, but reflect the needs of all men and women.
My anger is the anger that divides people from each other.
My resentment is the kind that causes men to destroy their
    neighbors.
My greed is the sort that leads to selfish disregard
    of the needs of others.
I am not as different as I like to pretend I am.
So when I ask for your forgiveness, I must forgive.
When I claim mercy, I must show mercy.
When I affirm faith in your grace,
  I must live graciously in relation to others.
You know, O Lord, this is not always easy for me to do.
Will you help me?
Will you give me more of the spirit of him whom we call Master?

Let me face the day that is ahead
  with courage and confidence in the future,
  with thankfulness for all the good things
   I have known and experienced,
  and with joy even amid tears
   that where I am and as I am,
 I am in your keeping.
I give myself into that keeping
  along with those I love. *Amen.*

I NEED TO LISTEN

How strange it is, O Lord,
    that I should feel I need to ask you to hear me.
Is it not I who need to learn to listen?
Should I not ask you to jerk me to my feet,
        to snatch me out of my drowsy indifference,
        to nudge me into alertness?
I am constantly surrounded by sounds I do not hear,
        by voices to which I am indifferent.

This is a singing world.
There are voices of angels
        and voices of lovers
        and voices of those inviting me to gladness everywhere.
Enable me to hear them, I pray,
    and in the hearing be lifted up to gratitude
        for the mystery and magic of being human.

This is a sobbing world.
There are voices filled with echoes of hurt and pain everywhere.
There are voices almost choked out by tears
        and voices that come out of aching.
There are hollow voices, empty voices.
I would rather not hear them—
        the voices of hungry children
        and of sorrowing women
        and of desperate men.
But they are all around me.
Enable me to hear them, I pray,
        and in the hearing
    be able to identify my brothers and sisters.

This is a shouting world.
There are voices of rage and of protest,
        of defiance and of contempt.
How carefully I sift out the shouting,
        ignore the screaming.
Make me listen, O God, I pray.
For you are the Father of us all,
        and sometimes the voices of anger carry messages from you.

Enable me to be a listener, I ask.
For in listening I may find direction and guidance.

Help me to listen to myself—
    to still, small voices of conscience,
    to whispers of faith,
    and to the soft inner humming of hope.

Help me to learn to trust myself more than I do,
    trust myself not because I am wise and good,
        but because I am loved and wanted.

I remember how the Lord Jesus spoke of your love for me
    and went all the way to a cross to show its meaning.
Help me to listen to others—
    to the person who is trying to tell me he loves me,
       and the person who is trying to tell me
          he needs my love in return.
Help me to listen to the stranger who may be an angel in disguise,
    to the friend who may be lonely and lost.
Help me to listen to the angry and the outraged
    who may be saying to me words I need to hear.

Steady me, O God, as a listener.
And when I speak, make me careful lest I use words as weapons
    and language as a severing sword.
Enable me to sort out what I hear
    and not be thrown off balance
       by the careless tongues of others.
Teach me to realize that just because a lie is spoken over and over,
    it does not become true.
Just because a falsehood is spoken loudly,
    it does not become less false.
So when prejudice and passion weight the words I hear
    with divisiveness and conflict,
    give me sense enough to reject them.
Give me judgment and common sense to cut through words
    that evade and distort lest I be misled.
Steady me, O Lord, as I learn to listen. *Amen.*

I NEED HELP WITH MY ROUTINE

I know, O God, that habit and routine
    can make reality come alive.
I live by habit and routine.
Much of my life is ordinary and uninspired.
Then suddenly out of habit meaning bursts!
Out of routine a glory comes!
For a moment I know life is good and you are real.
So I proceed along the way,
    poking and prodding at life,
    laughing and weeping,
    smiling and scowling.
Keep pushing meaning at me
    and prodding me with glimpses of glory,
  for I am nearsighted
    and so apt to overlook the good things
      that are at hand.
You surround me with opportunities to love and to serve.
You give me the stuff of life—
    food, books, work,
    wonder, beauty, dreams.
When the going is hard,
  you give me courage, comradeship, hope.
You give me times to pray and times to praise,
    times to complain and times to be thankful.

You have given me a big, wide, wonderful, awful world
    in which to live.
I see desolation and destruction on every hand,
    madness and meanness,
    cruelty and coldness.
I see also helpfulness and kindness,
    acceptance, tolerance, and goodness,
    occasionally even greatness among men.
Help me to identify evil for what it is
    and to identify myself with goodness
      wherever it is to be found. *Amen.*

I NEED STEADINESS

Almighty God,
I often become so lost in the fog of aimless living
    that I cannot feel life or see beauty
        or believe in faith and hope and love.
I often draw aside and live in loneliness and isolation.
I try to make up for what I feel instinctively
    I am missing in life by frantic striving for possessions,
        by persistent pursuit of pleasure.
I use life
    or at least try to use it.
I do not let life fill me;
    I try to fill it.
I remain at cross purposes with the real meaning of being alive.
I even try to manipulate you.
I want you to make up for my deficiencies,
        to compensate for my lack of willingness
            to take our Lord Jesus Christ seriously.
He calls me to openness of heart and fullness of life,
    and I am afraid to be openhearted,
        afraid someone may take advantage of me.
He calls me to faith in life
    and I am afraid to trust.
Something bad may happen.
He calls me to love
    and of that, above all, I am afraid.
I have been hurt,
I have been betrayed.
I do not want to reveal myself again.
So I build my shell and erect my little fortress of pride and disdain.
I will not be caught out again.
O God of the loving heart,
    can I trust you?
Can I count on you?
Will you stand by me when the darkness closes in?
Will you support me when the road is hard to travel?
Will you make the sunlight brighter and the nighttime bearable?
Are you really the God of all of life?
Help me now to accept your Presence and to discern your nearness.

I am apt to feel deserted when difficulties arise
    and lost when troubles come.
I am even tempted to blame you when things go wrong
  as though you were supposed to give me special treatment
    and protection from the adventure of being human.
Deliver me from making selfish demands
    and from expecting favored treatment.
Instead, steady me and hold me amid my perplexities.
Keep me loyal to the truth I know
    and let me not forget my best moments.

Deliver me from the feeling that I can make it on my own.
I need you.
Stay with me, I pray. *Amen.*

I AM NOT SURE OF LOVE

O Lord, I live in a world of angry men and women.
I am often angry myself at threats to my values,
    at brutal disregard for the institutions I hold dear.
Where do I belong in such a world?
Where does the Lord Jesus belong?
Is love weak,
    too weak to be creative?
Is compassion sheer sentiment?
Is this a time to be hard and tough?
My emotions tell me so some of the time.
Then at other times I see him moving
        amid the shadows of history.
I see him angry, too,
        at evidences of injustice
            and mistreatment of his fellow men.
I hear him lash out
        at self-righteousness and complacency.
I watch him at last,
        when the anger is done and the sharp words said,
    stake his life on love and self-sacrifice.
I behold him die and hear him say,
        "Father, forgive them
        for they don't know what they're doing."
And, somehow, O God,
    deep inside me I know love is not weak;
        it is I who am weak.
Love is indomitable and irresistible.
Hate is weakness.
Vengeance is futile,
    and violence is self-defeating.

Help me, for it is hard
        to stand by what I do know deep inside.
It is so much easier to curse
        than to bless.
It is easier to pronounce maledictions
        than to pronounce benedictions.
It is easier to shout others down
        than to sit down with others.

It is easier to be loud
    than to listen.
O God of all people,
    who does not separate us into good and bad
        but into loving and unloving,
  I need your help lest I tear things up.
You have offered to help me, I know,
    and I hold back.
Can you push a little harder?
I want to be more loving,
    and I am afraid.

Hear my prayer.
Make my commitment to love
    more than good intentions. *Amen.*

I FEEL DISCOURAGED

Almighty and Eternal God,
I come in prayer out of my needs, my moods, my desires.
Secret hurts and hopes mark me,
And I am fearful of exposing too much of myself to others.
 I might be laughed at or scorned.
 I might feel the weight of disapproval or rejection.
I hold back from others,
 but in your Presence I am still and waiting.
I know that your Spirit moves deep within my heart,
 that I cannot hold back from you.
Nor need I try.
For your love is greater than my transgressions,
 and your concern is limitless.
You are not shocked by my most carefully disguised feelings
 nor overwhelmed by my most unacceptable desires.
Work within me and move upon my heart.
I am aware that some prayers
 that surge to the surface of my feelings
 cannot be answered in the way I want them answered.
Help me to live with the "No" life sometimes speaks to me.
I am aware that I cannot manipulate life
 into the form I want it to take,
 nor fashion my existence
 into the shape I would like.
But keep me from despair or cynicism or bitterness.
There are rich experiences open to me every day.
There is love that can be given and received.
There is faith that can transform the ordinary.
There is hope in which I may walk.
I would give myself to your guiding Spirit
 in trust that love is never wasted,
 faith is never pointless,
 hope is never futile.
If tomorrow is uncertain,
 you are not. *Amen.*

I NEED TO ADMIT MY NEED

Almighty God, let me feel that I am praying,
  not just listening to words that fade into the silence.
Let me feel that I am reaching out
    into that greater dimension of reality
  wherein I live and move and have being.
Let me feel that somehow
  I am in touch with Someone more than I,
    who gives meaning to my little life
      and direction to my spirit.
Let me truly pray.

Let me truly pray as I acknowledge my dependence upon you.
I confess that I have often forgotten that dependence.
Now I am a bit frightened at what I have done.
I would like to undo some of it if I could.
The problem is it will be costly to undo it,
  and I must change some of my way of living.
You know, O Lord, how hard that is for me.
I find it difficult to give up even those things
    that are harmful and obviously destructive.
I keep blundering along in hope that somehow
    things will turn out differently
  from the way I fear they will.

I find it hard to admit I have been wrong
    even when I know it.
I find it hard to give up old animosities.
I find it hard to change,
  harder even than to keep compounding errors
    and complicating failures.
I find it easier to make excuses
    than to ask forgiveness.
I find it easier to curse
    than to bless.
I find it easier to hold others at arm's length
    than to put my arms around them.

O Lord, it is not because I am happier
  when I am at odds with the world around me.

In fact, I am often miserable.
It is just that I do not quite trust
　　forgiveness and love and faith and all those things
　　　　the Lord Jesus talked about.
I speak of him as Master and Teacher
　　and worship you through him as the very Word of God.
But I must confess to the feeling
　　that somehow I cannot make it in life
　　　　by taking him too seriously.
I call him the Way,
　　but I walk very gingerly
　　and step very carefully
　　and follow very far behind him.

So help me to truly pray.
For if I do,
　　perhaps some of my values can be sorted out,
　　some of my bewilderment dissipated,
　　and some of my uneasiness dispelled.
I have people to love and help all around me.
I have exciting miracles at hand every day.
Help me to be open to these things.
Help me to be ready
　　for whatever changes I need to undergo. *Amen.*

I NEED TO START OVER

Hear me, my Father, as I pray.
Hear the beat of my heart,
   the pulse of my spirit,
   the words spoken,
   and the words unspoken.
Hear me and help me to sort out my life,
   seeing the good and the evil with clearer eyes.
Help me to sort out my loves,
   clinging harder to that which is creative
   and letting go that which pulls me down.
Help me to acknowledge my sins and admit my evil.
But help me also to accept your forgiveness,
   so that I do not go about beating my breast
      and bemoaning my failure.
Help me to rise above that perverted kind of pride
   that causes me to regard my sins as remarkable
      and myself as unusual.

My faults, I know when I am honest,
   are pretty much the same old tired sins
      people have always committed.
I have surrendered to lust
   and called it love.
I have practiced petty selfishness
   and called it principle.
I have acted with smug bigotry
   and called it courage.
There is not a magnificent, bold sin among the lot.
But, O Lord, keep me from dwelling on that
   as though my very shabbiness can be a source of comfort.
For if I am shabby in my sins,
   you are magnificent in forgiveness.
If I am petty in my prejudices,
   you are splendid in your understanding.

So let me rise up and be done with the past.
Each day is new and fresh,
   and each hour is fraught with grandeur.

The world and life are full of wonder.
These are the things I would claim.
Hear me as I ask to be moved out from under
    the dripping skies of self-pity and self-blame
      into the sunlight of your love.
I've roads to walk
  and hills to climb
    and meadows in which to dance.
I've songs to sing
  and love to be shared
    and days and nights of fiery splendor on ahead.
Glory be to you, O God,
  for tender and tempestuous hours yet to come.

True it is,
  there may be dark places and rain clouds and starless nights.
I've known such experiences, O Lord,
  but I've seen them through so far by your grace.
There are tears to be shed and pain to be endured,
  but if you'll help me, I can make it.
Hear me as I ask that such things may be put in perspective.
Help me put myself in perspective,
  the kind of perspective Jesus gives
    when I stand alongside him. *Amen.*

I NEED TO FORGIVE AND BE FORGIVEN

If one asks him, "What are these wounds on your back?"
he will say, "The wounds I received in the house of my friends."
—Zechariah 13:6

O Lord, I come to my prayers with an open wound
    that is difficult to heal.
It was inflicted by my friend.
I have been wounded before,
But somehow the thrusts of an enemy do not leave the marks
    that the wounds of a friend leave.
The scars that remain longest
    are the ones we receive
  in the houses of our friends, our families, our lovers.
Scars inflicted by opponents heal over and fade.
The cutting words of someone about whom we care little
    may slice into our egos and rankle for a time.
But the cutting words of someone who matters to us
    slash to the bone and marrow of our very being.
O Lord, now in my praying,
    I look back upon hurts received and hurts given.
And in your Presence, I realize it is the latter
    that matter most.
Forgive me for the wounds I have inflicted,
    the hurts I have given to people whom I've loved.
Is it possible they are still glad they knew me ?
Do they remember shining moments of love and sharing
    that overshadow those darker times
      of misunderstanding and estrangement?
It would seem, O Lord, that we human beings,
    in our touching of others,
  are always hurting as well as helping,
    wounding as well as healing.
In the totality of any love there is pain.
Help me by your Spirit to learn to touch others
    with gentler hands and with trembling fingers.
Keep me from being so clumsy as to inflict needless wounds.

And when I err,
    when I misinterpret,
        when I fail to heed the messages that come from those I love,
Forgive me.
When I gash someone,
    whether carelessly or out of my own wounded spirit,
    make me quick to see what I have done
        and ready to say, "I'm sorry."
You have forgiven me so much, O God,
Forgive me this—
    the wounds received by others
        in my house of love. *Amen.*

I WANT TO UNDERSTAND MYSELF

O God, you are unfathomable mystery,
    ineffable and illimitable.
When I use such words,
    I am confessing my inadequacy in comprehension.
I call you Almighty God,
    Everlasting Father,
        Creator and Redeemer.
When I have done, the mystery remains
    and your being is clothed in a final darkness.
Yet is not life itself a mystery?
And are not our own human beings clothed in darkness?
There is the brilliance of sight and sound,
        the sharp intensity of feeling and touching,
        the magic of giving and receiving.

I do not understand myself.
I do not understand my responses to the world around me.
Why am I pushed to the brink of tears
    by a strain of music?
Why does my heart race
    to the rhythm of a poem?
Why am I near to bursting
    at some thing of beauty?
Why am I sad with another's sorrows
    and uplifted by another's joy?
Why am I so moved
    by the good things in life?
And why am I driven to doubt and despair at times
    by evil and ugliness?
Why do I keep trying to comprehend you
    and name you and seek you out?
Why, unless you are,
    and your Spirit moves me to seek you?
I know that whenever I give up the search,
    bleakness sets in and life stares me down
        with empty, haunted eyes.

O Lord, let me never lose
   the eager hope for fresh understanding.
Let me never lose
   the willingness to doubt and re-examine
      the understanding I feel I already have.

Renew my faith in the essential goodness of life,
      in the meaning behind words
         like faith and hope and love.
Let me see life as it is.
I do not want to be relieved
   of the necessity for facing reality.
I know what pain and suffering,
      betrayal and loss, can mean.
But deliver me from the bankrupt business
   of making a profession of sneering at goodness,
   of making a career out of uttering
      bright, brittle, cynical remarks
      about the meaninglessness of it all.
Give me the courage to work steadily
      for the best I can imagine
      amid the worst that I experience. *Amen.*

I REMEMBER

Eternal God, I am remembering.
Be with me in these moments.
I remember shining moments of happiness
    and shimmering moments of pain.
I remember times when belief was easy
    and times when faith came hard.
I remember hours when I exulted in the goodness of life,
    and long, slow, gray days
    when I clung to life's meaning by my fingertips.
I remember the ebb and flow,
    the pull and tug of life.
And I remember how often
    amid the shapelessness of my existence
    your Spirit seemed to move,
        giving form and structure to daily experiences.
I remember.
I marvel.
I am grateful.

O Lord, you hang rainbows amid the rain,
    mix dark green leaves with white magnolia blossoms,
    stir crimson streaks into sunset gold,
And I find my mingled memories
    are bitter-sweet and sad-glad.
So much of life is entangled,
    interwoven,
        a blending of light and dark.
Simplicity merges into complexity
    as understanding drifts into bewilderment.
I cannot ask to have it all assorted out for me, O God.
I do ask that as I remember past happiness and hurt,
    old loves and losses,
        once-upon-a-time achievements and satisfactions,
I may be drawn to a deeper appreciation
    of the multi-splendored opportunities my life has known.
Because I have known so much
    and experienced so much,
I can look ahead without panic.

So I go into today remembering—
   remembering your Spirit strives within us,
   remembering grace and courage are available,
   remembering where I've been and how it was.
If the present seems too unstable to trust
   and the future impossible to discern,
Uphold me on my memories. *Amen.*

I NEED TO FEEL THE SPIRIT

Ah God, I would thank you for your constant comings.
Sometimes I'm happy, sometimes I'm blue.
I fluctuate and vacillate.
Sometimes my heart sings, sometimes it sobs.
But your Spirit comes—
    sometimes when I pray for the coming,
    sometimes when I least expect it.

At times the Spirit moves in my life.
And I only realize as I look back
    that you were there in a special way,
        that the strength I had to resist a temptation,
        the assurance and comfort I felt at a dark time,
        the gladness I found around the bend of a lonely road,
    all were results of your coming to me unexpectedly.

Keep coming, O Lord,
For I often get too busy,
    too harried,
        too preoccupied with the details of everyday living
    to feel the wind of the Spirit.
I need to stop and look up
    and see the leaves hang trembling
    far more often than I do.
Perhaps I will be more aware from now on,
    perhaps not.
So keep coming, Lord.
I desperately need you. *Amen.*

I AM LONELY

God of people,
You are represented in the Bible as speaking to people,
     even carrying on conversations.
Is that the way some long-ago poet had of dreaming
    that maybe you get lonely too?
O Lord, if that is an impious idea,
    forgive me for it.
It just comes to mind
    because I am so much that way.
I need times of solitude and privacy
But if I were not able to hear voices
     other than my own occasionally,
    and see faces,
    and bump up against people,
I do not think I could make it.

Yet I know I am not ever alone,
    not really.
For you are always near.
That is why I speak out loud to you now and then.
At times I think I would like for you to answer back,
    but if you did, I would die of fright.
It comforts me to believe you hear me,
    even if it is best that you do not answer.
Or do you? *Amen.*

I WILL SING A NEW SONG

Lord God,
Yesterday I sang a sad song of an old love.
I felt mellow and nostalgic and lonely.
Then something within me,
    some prodding spirit from you,
   made me look around me
     at all the fresh beautiful things
      that have come into my life.
My heart began to fumble for a melody
    and for words to express my feelings.
That was but yesterday, O Lord.

Today, somehow the fresh beautiful things
     have come surging back,
  and I am very grateful.
I want to sing a new song.
I want to set the fresh beautiful things to music.
I want to find words with which to praise you
    who are the Giver.
I want a tune with a lilt and a lift to it.
I want it to ring with "Alleluias"
    and set my feet to dancing.
I know one day the new song may seem like a sad song again,
    of old loves and half-remembered joys.
But when that time comes,
  I'll be asking for another new song.

Is that what the joy of faith means:
    new songs for new days,
  songs that keep reminding us
    that life is never over, never done?
There are always fresh beautiful things
    to be discovered, cherished, and set to music. *Amen.*

I AM GROWING OLDER

He restores my soul.
—Psalm 23:3

O God, I am glad you don't just put me back
    in the shape I once was.
I confess that I would not want to be restored
      to the callowness of my youth,
      to the thoughtless complacency of my early life.
The very experiences that have marred me and scarred me
      and given my life its weatherbeaten qualities
    are the experiences through which I have come to be
      so deeply conscious of your grace.
I ramble through the ramshackle rooms of my memory
    and see the walls you've knocked down
      at one time or another of restoration.
I recall how you rewired my spirit with forgiveness,
      not just once but again and again.
You have redone me so many times,
    refurbished me within,
      refurnished my thinking,
    even redecorated me
      in a way that made my heart skip with joy.
And I'm wiser, I think,
    gentler, I think,
      less judgmental of others, I think,
And closer to you, I hope.
For in each restoration
    I find how much needs restoring.

Thank you for not making me into what I once was,
    for not just giving me a paint job on the outside.
I'm grateful that you've spared no expense
    in your restoration work among us humans,
Even though it cost you Jesus Christ. *Amen.*

I NEED TO BE STILL

Eternal God,
Help me to be still for a few moments.
Of all things hard,
   stillness seems to be hardest for me.
My life is filled with clanging and clattering.
At times I deliberately create noise to fill the silence.
I turn on the radio,
   talk to myself,
      seek places where hubbub reigns.
Even in the church I prefer sound at all times—
      the organ, the choir, the minister's voice.
Nor can I be motionless very long.
I am a go-go person,
      always on the move, bustling and busy,
    falling into bed exhausted and rising in the morning
      to rush through the day.

Why is this, O Lord?
Is it because I cannot stand myself?
Or is it because I have been taught
   to associate life with loudness and achievement with busyness?
Help me now to be still for a while.
Steady my jumpy nerves
   and calm my quivering spirit.
Let me look inward upon myself
   and meet you in the deep places of my heart.
I know I need not be afraid,
For when you come,
   it is with healing, restoration, forgiveness.

I know I cannot stay still.
I must move again.
I have little things to do,
   people with whom I must talk,
      places to go.
But out of this time of stillness,
   help me to go steadier and surer.
Give me a feeling for prayer in motion,
   for thoughts flung out toward eternity.

I wonder if I am afraid you cannot move as fast as I move
    or hear my prayers above the everyday clatter of my life.
I know such fears are foolish.
You remain beside me.
You heed even my unspoken desires and hopes.
Be with me as I go. *Amen.*

I ASK "THY WILL BE DONE"

God, my God,
I would praise you in prayer, but how?
Across the surface of my mind random thoughts slide.
I cannot organize them or sort them all out.
I fall back upon "Now I lay me down to sleep,"
But it is not bedtime,
   and, besides, that will not do for an adult.
I say "Our Father, My Father, who art in heaven."
I say it knowing that I often feel like an orphan of the storm.
I say "Hallowed be thy name,"
   knowing how frequently I treat your creation
     in unhallowed fashion.
I pray "Thy kingdom come."
Suppose it did.
Where would I fit into a kingdom of love?
Is there a corner in which I might sit
   with my limited ability to love,
     my prejudices and my facile judgments
       upon my fellow human beings?

"Thy will be done?" I ask.
Why should I say "thy will," O God?
Why do we humans so often infer
   that "thy will" is dark and foreboding,
     suppressing our natural desires,
       curtailing our enjoyments of life?
Is not "thy will" liberating and freeing?
Does not "thy will" encompass joy and exhilaration,
     buoyancy and zest in life?
"Thy will" must embrace the world of sense and sight and sound
     in which you have placed us.
It may even be that "thy will" frequently is "my will"
     when I feel most myself.
At those times when I move toward life,
   allow myself the thrill of being,
     the naturalness of reaching out to others,
     the enjoyment of beauty and feeling,
Am I not in accord with "thy will"?

And in those dark moments when I must simply wait it through,
  hanging on and hanging in,
Do I not fulfill "thy will' for me by knowing
      that your grace is sufficient for me
    and the excitement of loving and living will return?
"Thy will be done." *Amen.*

I NEED A SENSE OF PEACE

Give me peace, O God, a central peace.
   Let me know that at the heart of turbulence
   there is the final calm that comes from faith in you,
     that at the core of life
   there is the great confidence
     whence come courage and gladness.
When I leave my private place of prayer,
   let me go with the assurance
     that I carry within that central peace
       that no agitation can shake.
Give me a standing place in life
   wherefrom I may be able to look steadily
     upon my world without panic.
I see the divisions among human beings
   and hear the shouts of hatred and anger.
Keep me from giving into the mad idea
     that peace among your children is impossible.
Keep me from being content with things as they are.
Out of my central peace,
   let there ripple forth concern and compassion,
     indignation at injustice,
   and a willingness to give of myself
     in the spirit of Christ.

I come, O Lord God, out of my own need
   and my own hope.
May I attain the feeling
   that I have touched that central peace
     which abides amid the confusion of life. *Amen.*

PRAYERS FOR UNCOMMON DAYS

FOR AN AVERAGE SUNDAY

Eternal God, look now upon me as I wait,
  stilled for a time,
    subdued and quiet.
You know that it is hard for me to wait,
It is hard for me to be still.
I rush from one thing to another,
  churning up my life
    into hectic waves of accomplishment.
When night falls, I confess I feel a bit guilty
  if I have done nothing except be myself.
I even come to prayer with the feeling
  that it is apart from life,
  that when it is over I had best do something.
Even in church I want to sing a hymn
  or take up an offering.
And then when church is over,
  I plunge back into my world where the action is.
O Lord, do I have it wrong,
  twisted around?
Are there more occasions than I realize
  when I would be a better person
  if I didn't do anything but just stand there?
Do I fail to hear the real needs
  of loved ones, friends, and neighbors,
  because I am too busy figuring out
    what next to do for them,
      or maybe to them?
Am I so absorbed in running the world
  that I am not aware of you
    and of the things you have to say to me?
Calm me down, I pray.
Calm me down
    to the place where I can remember
  how many times you have managed to keep me going
    when I thought I could not make it.

Calm me down
   so that I can recall times of steadiness and fear
      when a courage was infused in me
         that enabled me to hold on.
Calm me down
   so that I can accept my limitations without panic
      and in the knowledge that I cannot do everything.
In many ways I do not do anything.
In some ways I do the wrong things.
In the silence before the mystery and the meaning,
I stand waiting,
   still,
      quieted by wonder.
For life is filled with mystery, meaning, and wonder.
The mystery of being itself.
The meaning that keeps breaking through to me,
   meaning encompassed in words
      like faith, hope, and love.
And I wonder why when I pray, I believe,
   and why when I believe, I pray.
May I be assured that what I do matters
   and what I say counts,
Because you are in me and for me.
Through Jesus Christ our Lord. *Amen.*

FOR AN APRIL DAY

April is the cruellest month ...
            —T. S. Eliot

O Lord of April,
    of the spring rains and the dull roots,
    of lilacs and memory,
    of the dead land and of desire,
Hear me as I pray out of my memories and my desires.
Hear me and wash me clean
    as the spring rains wash the earth.
Hear me and stir my hopes and renew my faith in life.
I am overwhelmed with April,
    with her showers and her sun,
    with her cruelty and her promise.
But then,
    so much of life is April.

So much of living is a matter
    of "breeding lilacs out of the dead land."
There are long-ago dreams that come back to me in the night
    and far-away hopes that beckon me in the sun.
There are memories that hurt
    and recollections of things past that will not let me go.
There are ancient promises unkept,
    desires unrealized,
        high purposes unfulfilled.
Now and then they are warmed
        by the sun of my good intentions
    and stirred
        by the spring rain of resolution.
I mean to rise again
    and walk straight and tall under the sky,
but I dawdle and drift,
    and April is gone.
I have people to love and kind words to speak.
I have songs to sing and prayers to pray.
I have letters to write and "thank you's" to say.

I have a wrong that needs correcting,
   an apology to make,
      a hand to hold out.
I have so many things to do.
Stir my dull roots of irresolution,
O Lord of April, hear my prayer. *Amen.*

FOR A WINTER DAY

How beautiful is our world, O Lord,
  and how marvelous are your ways in it.
You draw splendor out of the barrenness of winter.
You create magnificence amid the starkness and desolation
    of cold rains and morning fogs.
You make hearts to sing
  long after the angel hosts have gone
    and left the skies empty and silent.
You place dabs of riotous color
  amid the drabness of desert places.

You come into my plain life and make it shine—
    when I let you.
My problem lies here so often—
    in the letting.
For I am grim and stubborn sometimes.
I refuse to believe that you are here.
I slam doors and lock windows and brood alone.
I think upon the barrenness,
  ponder the desolation,
    enjoy the drabness.
It gives me something to complain about.
It enables me to ask, "Where is God?
  Look at me, deserted and bereft."
O God, forgive me
  for I know now what I do when I shut you out:
I turn sour within.
I find I cannot love my neighbor or accept myself.
I sink into self-pity
  and contemplate the ways in which life has abused me.

You know that there is ugliness
  as well as beauty in our world.
You know that winter comes to the heart
  as well as to the world of nature.
You know that I must live with the oak trees stripped of leaves
    and the magnolias bare of blossoms.
You know about the cold rains
    and the winter fogs that fall upon my spirit.

But you are here.
Help me to hang on when hanging on is hard.
Help me to remember
  the rhythm of life is often like the rhythm of the seasons.
Camellias will bloom once more,
  roses will be back,
    the jasmine will scent the night air,
And spring will come.
How can I doubt it?

Draw splendor out of me,
Color my life red and gold.
Make my spirit sing and my feet dance.
Guide me through the cold rain and the morning fog.
Let me love the many faces of your world
  and not be afraid of that which is strange and new.
Let me love in order that I may truly live,
  and live in order that I may love. *Amen.*

FOR A DAY OF PUBLIC CALAMITY

How often, O Lord,
  do I read casually of disasters afar?
How often, O Lord,
  do I hear indifferently of catastrophes far removed?
Then when disaster moves close to me
    when catastrophe shatters the calm of my life,
  I come alive to pain and loss.
I know you understand how limited I am,
    by my love that fades off into indifference,
    by the boundaries of my friendships and personal concerns.
I am just that way.
So come to me now as I pray for the stricken,
    for those who grieve and mourn.
Perhaps I will be more sensitive in the future,
    more aware,
      a bit gentler and kinder.
For all of us move along the razor's edge between life and death.

Give me a greater appreciation of life and love and other people.
Draw me closer to those whom I profess to love.
Give me the will to be more helpful
    and more aware of others' needs.
In the face of the mystery of life and death,
  give me courage to trust your sustaining daily presence.
Let me not forget that in life and death
  all of us are yours.

I pray for all your children,
    for men and women who live in pain,
      physical and emotional,
    for those who seek and cannot seem to find,
    for those who live confidently
      and yet need that something more
        which comes from fellowship with you in Christ.
I pray for all well and happy people,
    that in their fullness of life
  they may know the abundance that comes through Christ.

We all need your Spirit, O God,
    not just in times of calamity,
  but also in our days of strength and well-being.

So I call upon you, O Lord, in this day of trouble.
In my calling, may I hear your voice saying,
  "Lo, I am with you always." *Amen.*

FOR THE MORNING AFTER A STORM

O Lord, who rides the storm
    and whose coming is like the wind,
  I give you thanks.
I can recall last night's rain driving silver lances
    in the light flung from the windows,
  last night's wind pushing, bending,
  last night's vivid lightning bolts illuminating black skies,
    then gone.
And now the morning is come—
    clear skies, moist earth, sweet air.
      "Morning has broken
    Like the first morning..."
Each of your mornings, O God,
    is like the first morning,
      a brand new beginning.
No, not really!
Like the first morning, yet unlike.
The memory of the srorm remains.
The aftermath of the storm is evident here and there—
  leaves and limbs beaten to the ground,
  a bit of debris scattered hither and yon,
  a little clutter that was not here before.

Like life, O Lord?
That is, like the life within each of us?
  the drumming pain,
  the pushing fear,
  the vivid remorse,
  the driving despair,
    whatever—
I knew these things last night
    or a thousand nights ago,
  and you have restored me and I am grateful.
I've a new morning,
    like the first morning of a long-ago innocence.
Yet it is unlike, O Lord,
  I know it is unlike.

The storms have left their reminders.
But it does not matter.
I do not have to go about the yard of my life
    picking up leaves and sticks.
I let them lie.
They are a part of the world I now know:
  some of them will molder into the ground,
  some of them will lie in view forever,
And other storms will come, I know.
Meanwhile, I you give thanks
    for this morning after the storm
      with my laundered world and my clear sky.
I can see better for a time,
  and that is enough. *Amen.*

FOR THE NIGHT BEFORE SURGERY

O Lord, I know I had better do my praying now.
In the morning they will sedate me and tranquilize me
    and anesthetize me and whisk me away in a fog.
I will see faces and hear voices
    but they will blend and merge into a haze.
So I pray.

I pray for the surgeon whose skill is so vital.
I pray for the nurses whose help is so important.
I pray for the anesthetist and all the support staff.
I know you work with and through them.
I pray for my loved ones who are anxious
    and who feel so helpless waiting in that Family Lounge.

I pray for me.
I confess that I am anxious.
Surely it would be unnatural
    not to feel a knot of apprehension deep inside.
I want to be well and strong again.
I am not asking you to guarantee that, O Lord.
I know such things cannot be guaranteed
    but I know you understand my wanting and you care.

So be with me even though I will be too far out of it to pray.
Be with those doctors and nurses
    even though they will be too busy to pray.
Now let me rest.
Somewhere one of the Psalmists said of you,
    "He gives his loved ones sleep."
Thank you, God,
    and I'll say "Goodnight" instead of Amen.

FOR THE BIRTH OF A DAUGHTER

God, we thank you that she is beautiful,
    with her squinched up eyes and her tiny, tiny toes.
She is beautiful because she is ours,
    or so we think now.
Yet from the beginning we must start giving her up
    so that she can be herself.

We must love her but not smother her.
We must care for her and protect her
    but not keep her too close.
We want her to live and love and be herself.
We know that she will experience hurt and heartache
    that we cannot prevent.
She will also find beauty,
    hear an inner music,
        and walk on the wind.

Right now she seems completely and dependably ours.
We are glad to know such a feeling.
Touch her and us with the finger of your Spirit
So that in our life together
    we may enrich each other. *Amen.*

FOR THE BIRTH OF A SON

O Lord, he is here, wrinkles and all,
    and we are grateful.
We are grateful because he has made it
    through the trauma of birth,
        with his ten fingers and ten toes,
            two eyes, a mouth and a nose.
So he is here, and we are grateful.

Let us never forget this moment of excitement.
Let us never forget how we feel now, thinking "Miracle!"
For he will turn out to be unmiraculous.
He will keep us awake at night.
He will tire us by day.
He will stamp his feet and cry.
We will have to be stern with him at times.
We may even spank him.

Some day he will grow up and go away
    and part of each of us will go with him.
That will be a miracle too,
    a miracle of love and life,
        our miracle,
The ongoing miracle of the way we humans are saying Yes
    to your world of ecstasy and pain,
        of loving and being loved. *Amen.*

FOR A WEDDING ANNIVERSARY

O Lord, we are grateful for a day of celebration.
Another year has gone by with its experiences —
    good, bad, and indifferent.
We are together and thankful for our togetherness.
Through our life with each other
  we have so much for which to be thankful.
We have known all the intricate intimacies
    of two people learning to live together.
We have shared secrets together and have realized
  there are private places in each of us
    the other can never know.
We have known the ecstasy of physical union
    and the relief of temporary apartness.
We have quarreled and quickly made up.
We have quarreled and not made up
    until we realized
  that life without the other was empty.
We have laughed with each other
    and at each other.
We have prayed together.
We have learned how words can cut and wound
    and how words can soothe and comfort.
We have learned too
  that there are times when it is better to be silent.
We have felt upon occasion that our love was eternal,
    and wondered at times
  if our marriage would last another week.
We have run the whole gamut of human emotions and feelings.
So, gratefully, O God, we celebrate it all—
    the loving and the sharing,
    the anger and the frustration,
    the giving and the taking,
    the fire and the ashes.
Bless by your Presence the renewal of our promise
  and our covenant,
    in joy and in sorrow,
    in plenty and in want,
    in sickness and in health,
  as long as we both shall live. *Amen.*

FOR A DAY OF REMEMBRANCE

You have called me, O God,
    to privileges and opportunities.
You have made me in your image
    and placed within me the mark of your likeness.
You have given me feelings and emotions,
    rational processes and the will to choose
        what I shall do with your gifts.
You have given me so many things,
    and I am grateful.

You have given me memories to hold,
    and I cherish that which I have known and loved.
You have taught me how to keep alive
        the lingering poetry of time and place.
You have enabled me to recall the green of spring
    when winter comes,
    and the lushness of summer when December is barren and cold.
You have given me the memory of faces and voices,
    the remembrance of hands once touched,
        and laughter and tears once shared.
I am thankful for all good memories this day —
        for people I have known,
        for streets I have walked,
        and for houses I have lived in.
You have given me so much, O Lord,
    and I spend so little time remembering.
Yet I know you understand,
    for life goes on.
And to that end you have given me hope.
Sharpen my expectations this day, I pray.
Excite me to the end that
    I may look toward tomorrow with sunrise eyes.
Teach me that I am not just what I have been,
    I am also what I hope for.
Remind me that if my hopes are small,
    I am small.
If my faith is limited,
    my tomorrows are limited.

Take this squeezed-in heart of mine and expand it.
Take this choked-up voice of mine and enable me to shout:
   "Glory and honor be to the one God our Father,
      this day and always."

Set me on my way singing, O Lord.
Let me remember that your truth is known,
      not in lessons memorized once long ago
         nor in deeds done once,
      but in the continuing Presence of the Holy Spirit.
Let me remember yesterday,
   and let me anticipate tomorrow.
Through Jesus Christ our Lord. *Amen.*

FOR THE DAY AFTER A FUNERAL

That one I loved, O God,
  is now with you.
I can say that,
    not knowing "how" or "where,"
  but say it because it makes no sense
    that so rich and full a life
      would come to an abrupt end . . .
  except for memories.
Still, I am bereft for she is not with me.
I listen to all the clichés of my friends,
    spoken to console me:
  "She is better off."
  "She is past her pain and suffering."
  "She is in heaven," whatever that means.
I listen and am not consoled.
My grief is selfish.
I want to feel her touch
  and hear her voice
    and see her smile.
I am confident she is with you,
  amd I am just as confident, O Lord,
    you understand how it is with me.
I cannot help recalling times
  I might have been gentler, softer, more thoughtful.
I wish I could live some hours over.
I would like to say "I love you" just one more time.
These failures I must accept.

"Time heals all things," they say.
I do not believe Time does anything.
You, O God, are Healer and Helper.
You can heal me in time,
  help me through the lonely days and long nights.
You can give me renewed zest for going on
    and entering into life once more.

"Thanks be to God who gives us the victory
through our Lord Jesus Christ."
I believe that.
But right now I grieve; I hurt; I am bereft.
Thanks be to God who understands
through Jesus Christ our Lord. *Amen.*

FOR THANKSGIVING DAY

"I will praise the name of God with a song:
I will magnify him with thanksgiving."
So wrote the Psalmist long ago.
I am grateful, O Lord, for all the impulses to praise you
    which come to me in life.
Even in the discouragement of some situation
        wherein I feel helpless and totally inadequate,
    I feel the impulse to grow and do the best I can.
Amid the pain and hurt that life can bring,
    I find the solace and comfort that come to me
        from friends and loved ones.
Just at the time I feel most alone,
    there are evidences of the concern of others
        and assurances of your Presence.
I am not always conscious of these realities, God.

I even become impatient at times
        when I hear words of faith spoken
            and songs of hope sung.
I withdraw from the life around me,
    take pity upon myself for my misfortunes,
        and feel no desire to praise.
Then I am startled into new awareness
        by a flower,
        a song,
        a persistent friend,
        a gift,
        a smile.
Almost in spite of myself I am lifted up
        and lifted out into thanksgiving.
        and life begins again.

I am thankful, O God,
    that you keep prodding me
        and pushing me into joy and celebration.
I am thankful for spoken words and silent gestures,
        for laughter and outstretched hands,
        for back-door mercies and winding graces
            that enwrap me.

I am thankful for tangible and measurable things,
     for churches and hospitals,
     for schools and homes.
I am grateful for ancient words that come alive once more.
     "Sing aloud, O daughter of Zion; shout O Israel!
     Rejoice and exult with all your heart . . . . "
I am thankful for the music of the heart
     and for the music of the human voice.
As I praise you this day,
   I am grateful for the rich beauty of songs sung
     and the warm impulses with which I respond.
I will praise your name, O Lord, with a song.
I will magnify you with thanksgiving.
     Through Jesus Christ our Lord. *Amen.*

FOR THE DAY I BEGIN MY CHRISTMAS SHOPPING

O God, I do like real things
    like money and houses,
      fast automobiles and diamond rings.
Forgive me that when I think of Christmas,
  I often think of real things like that.
I teach my children to think
    of bicycles and dolls,
    of toy trains and airplanes,
    of sugar and spice and everything nice.
Forgive me for my foolishness.
These things I spend so much time playing around with are not bad,
  I can even use them creatively.
They make up much of my world
  and occupy a great deal of my time.
But you know what my problem is?
I get so involved in accumulating them
  that I forget who I am.
I get so surrounded by them
    that I end up tanglefooted,
  stumbling along from thing to thing,
  falling down at times,
  bruising my shins upon them.

Can you clear away some of the clutter
  of my life this year, O Lord?
Can you help me pick my way through the crowded stores?
Can you make me quiet long enough to hear angels?
Can your Word about life break through
  the blare of tawdry commercials,
The commercials that insist life can be bought
  if I will only go deeply into debt?

Lord, do you understand me?
Can you help me understand myself?
Do I really substitute gifts for self-giving too often?
Would I do better to say "I love you"
  as I pass out the presents?
Would I come closer to someone
  by spending as much time listening as I do shopping?

These thoughts bother me at times.
It may be that in my busyness
　　I am losing touch with the things that are most real.
It may be I am losing touch with you
　　and with the Child whom you sent
　　　　to grow up to be a Man,
　　whose word was your Word
　　　　and whose love was your Love.

I like real things,
　　and I know if I will listen,
I may hear of the most real things of all,
　　things like hope and love and faith,
　　　　that can change lives, even mine,
　　and renew them in the image of Christ my Lord. *Amen.*

FOR THE BEGINNING OF ADVENT

O Lord my God,
You have made me,
   and you have made this world in which I live.
I so often forget that you are Creator and Maker of all.
I set myself apart as though I were special,
   and as though I alone came from your hand.
I have a secret feeling that other men just happened,
   while I and those like me were created.
So I often try to convince myself that I am above the ordinary.

But when I come to this season of the year, O God,
   when I recall the coming of the Lord Jesus long ago
     and anticipate his renewed coming in glory,
   I am baffled and taken aback.
For I confess him Lord.
And yet he came,
   a member of a persecuted people
     far from our golden shores.
He was born in a stable amid the steamy fragrance of animals.
He was dark of skin and bare of possessions.
He was executed as a criminal on a crude cross.
He was called the Word made flesh.
I try my best to make him like me,
   but the facts will not let me.
Dare I try to be like him?

I cannot make myself over
   so that I am like him in skin texture and racial lineage,
     or even in his poverty.
I cannot become a wanderer as he was.
I cannot go back to a stable.
But perhaps these things do not matter.
I can be like him in spirit,
   and in his Spirit there was a bigness and a boldness
     that ignored the accidents of birth
       and the trappings of daily life.
In his Spirit he embraced all humanity.

I would like to do that.

But if that is too much for my little heart,

    deliver me at least from contemptuous rejection of others.

If I cannot love everybody,

    let me love a few people and treat all people with respect.

If I cannot even do that all year round,

    help me to do it in this Advent season. *Amen.*

FOR A SUNDAY IN ADVENT

Eternal God, I remember Jesus,
  the way he lived,
  the things he said,
  the assurances he gave.
I remember Jesus and what I know of you
    because of him.
I remember Jesus and how he died,
  and how he rose again.
I remember his living Presence in our world,
  and how I am reminded of him again and again.
I remember him especially during these days of Advent,
  his coming as the Child of Bethlehem
    through the strange miracle of his birth
      that hallows all births.
I remember, and the tight, taut tenseness
    with which I cling to my little world
  eases a little,
  and I am not quite as fearful,
    quite as defensive,
    quite as protective of my possessions and my position.
I even give a little—
  give a little of my money to church and charity,
    to the needy and the hungry.
I give a little to my friends and my family
    and feel quite good about it,
  even though most of the people to whom I give
    already have too much.
Yet there is meaning in the giving
    and love wrapped up in the present
      with its gaudy bows and pretty ribbons.
Forgive me, O Lord, that so much of my giving
  is measured by the price tag.

Is there someone this year for whom a bit of love in a box
    or a gesture of concern with a ribbon on it
  could mean even more than the present bought and paid for?
Is there a corner of my life I might give to someone or to you?
Is there a bundle of feelings that ought to be unwrapped?
If so, help me, I pray, as I remember Jesus
    and what he gave. *Amen.*

FOR A SUNDAY IN ADVENT

I remember the blue-cold child
  who came to a winter world, O God,
    wherein those who were warm and well-fed
  knew not of his coming.
I know that for many people
  our world is a winter world.
There are the starving and the wandering,
    the victims of famine and of war.
There are in our nation
  those who face the debilitating fear of unemployment
    and the terrible frustration of not being needed or wanted.
And the blue-cold child will come again on Christmas Day.
In my remembering him,
  Let me not forget them,
    the helpless and the hungry,
  those who either have no songs to sing
    or no strength for singing.
For in my remembering him, O Lord,
  I become aware that he was a hand reaching out
    to the whole world,
  he was a gift to all mankind.

He was the warm fire of your love in a winter world.
He was your arm reached out to embrace the lost and the lonely,
    the lovable and the unlovable.
And in remembering him,
  I recall my own identity as one who has taken his hand,
    warmed my heart at the fire of your love,
    entered the embrace of your concern.
I am grateful.
And then in your presence, O God,
  I ask myself if my gratitude spills over into other lives.
I must confess I am not sure it does,
  at least not very often.

So I pray this Advent that my remembering may become renewal,
  my recollection enlargement.

Go with me as I move through these December days
    toward the Christmas morning
        where again the blue-cold child will cry under the winter sky.
    I remember Jesus, O God,
    and in the memory is the mystery of love,
        your love and our love,
    all love divine and human.
And the mystery is the memory of life
    in Jesus Christ our Lord. *Amen.*

FOR A SUNDAY IN ADVENT

Glory to you, O God!
Peace on earth! Good will toward men!
My spirits sag, my voice stammers,
   as the angel song rings out once more.
For there is all too little of your glory to be discerned
     through the murky disarray of these times.
Surely, there is no peace on earth.
Good will is thinned out
  and spread lightly upon the surface
    of human relationships.
The nations growl at one another,
  and the peoples of the earth shudder
    beneath the threat of annihilation.
Will the spirit of peace and good will prevail, O Lord?
Will the nations beat swords into plowshares
  and spears into pruning hooks?
The hope comes surging back as the angels sing
    against the skies of Christmas once again.

But even as I hope once more,
  I examine myself.
And in the light of the Christmas star,
  my spirits sag to half-mast
    and my voice stammers into confession.
      of my own inadequacies.

I do not feel much glory in life right now.
I say "Merry Christmas,"
  but it lacks much of a shine.
I am harried and hurried,
  my nerves all ajangle.
I take a time of peace and sing about it,
    while my nervous system screams protest
      against the pressures of this season.
Sometimes even my good will is forced,
  and my jolly words are pushed through clenched teeth.
I wish the whole thing were behind me
  so that I could be my cranky, crotchety self again,
    without feeling guilty.

Yet when I stop to think,
I do not really wish it were all behind me.
I know there is a beauty I must not miss.
So relieve my mind and relax my tension
by your Spirit, O God.
Take the pressure off and let me feel the Presence
of the Child of Bethlehem. *Amen.*

FOR CHRISTMAS EVE

Eternal God, I wait now for Christmas.
I want the Christ to be born anew in my heart.
I hope it will all mean more to me than ever before.
Do not let it slip away into the night
   after the songs have all been sung
      and the stories told once more.
I know we cannot keep the expectancy alive the year round,
   but can I not keep the meaning warm?
Knowing myself, I ask now
   that the Christ Child may be real to me,
      not only in the days immediately ahead,
   but in the days that follow the celebration of his birth.
Let me so receive him that I may believe
      in his continuing Presence.
Let me not let love go.
Let me not let faith fade.
Let me not let hope slip away.
May openheartedness be my way of life,
   and an abiding joy be an aspect of my very being.

So involve me in the Coming this year
   that the going will not be quite as complete
      as it has been in the past.
Help me to remember what it is all about.
Keep my life from being so crowded with things
   that there is no room for him.
Keep me from pushing him aside and from being so busy
   that I lose him in the clutter and the clamor
      of these hectic days.

I am glad that Christmas means parties and decorated trees,
      wassail bowls and candles in the windows.
But let me remain aware that it also means
   generosity and forgiveness,
      openness and renewal.
It means commitment and restoration,
   worship and wonder.

It means the birth of our Lord,
and the Kingdom, the Power, and the Glory
of your love for all people everywhere.

So make me ready now,
and then when the candles have been extinguished,
and the trees taken down,
and the wreaths put away,
May the memory of the Lord Jesus remain
a present and transforming reality in my life.
For his sake I pray. *Amen.*

FOR NEW YEAR'S EVE

Eternal God, before whom we are creatures of the day
    and children of the hour,
I lift my prayers to you
  as I stand in the shadows of the waning year.
I am aware once more of the fleetingness of time,
    the transiency of my being.
So much has happened to me
  during the year now so rapidly slipping away,
So much of hurt and happiness,
    of loss and gain,
      of hope and fear.
I did not expect the sorrow that was thrust upon me.
I was surprised by the turn of events that changed my life.
I look back.
I remember how different life a year ago was.
The slow, quiet erosion of the days has gone on,
    and I am not quite the same person I was,
      for better or for worse.
I have had a whole year to grow in love
    or to fall out of love,
  to turn my hands to constructive tasks,
    or to turn away in idleness.
I have had a whole year,
  and now it is almost gone.
No matter what I have done or failed to do,
  O Lord, keep me from dwelling on it too much.
If I have failed,
  help me put my failure behind me.
If I have done well,
  help me to be glad but not complacent.
There are other hills to climb
    and new hopes to be realized.

I know, O God,
  you understand my need to look back for a while,
    wistfully peering at the past.
But start me looking forward.
I do not know what events are ahead,
  but I do know you are there,
    and I am grateful. *Amen.*

FOR MARDI GRAS

Lord God, Maker of this day,
   lift up my heart that I may rejoice and be glad.
For shining sun and cloudless skies,
For blooming camellias and blossoming trees,
   I rejoice and am glad.
For the exuberance of life,
For the exhilaration of festivals and fun,
   I am glad.
For laughter and beauty,
For glee and gladness,
   I rejoice.
This is a day which you have made.

I am grateful, O Lord, that there is no way
   in which I can fall outside your concern.
As I enter this time marked in our city by the hilarity of Mardi
     Gras,
   go with me.
If I laugh with those who laugh
   or stand aside with those
     for whom Mardi Gras is a day to be endured,
   be with me.
Let me not be too harsh on those who come among us seeking fun,
   some of them determined to have a good time.
All of us have some of that desperate need to be happy.
I need to discover gaiety and levity
   for those too are a part of the whole life.
Keep me, however, from forgetting
   that in the balance Mardi Gras needs Ash Wednesday
     when the parades have ended
       and the music has died
         and the balls are over and we are quiet again.
Help me to discover wholeness,
    the wholeness of being in you,
   God of gladness and of grief,
    of happiness and tears. *Amen.*

FOR ASH WEDNESDAY

O Lord, I ponder days when no sun shines
    and the clouds are dark and heavy overhead,
  when the flowers are dead
    and the trees are stripped bare by the wind.
Can I rejoice still and be glad?
I would rejoice,
  not with that surface joy
    that sometimes overlies my true feelings,
  but with deep-down joy
    that throbs through life in spite of pain.
I would be glad,
  not with the easy gladness of frivolity and mirth,
    but with the depth of gladness that rises at the heart of life.
For life, I know, moves along different ways for each of us.
Each of us knows times of exultation
    when life seems good and rich.
Each of us knows days of uncertainty
    when life seems to wobble and weave along an unmarked way.
We have lost the sun and we are chilled and anxious.
Those too are days of which we may say,
  "This is the day which the Lord has made.
  Let us rejoice and be glad . . . . "

Let me rejoice and be glad.
For I am aware, O God, that you have given me life
    in a world I cannot always manage.
I cannot control events and circumstances,
  nor can I escape involvement in human hurt and pain.
I cannot ward off illness and suffering
  either from my own life or from the lives of those I love.
But I can rejoice that each day brings the marks of your Presence.
I can be glad that nowhere is outside the circle of your care.

So keep me living, O Lord, not lopsidedly but wholly.
Keep me alive to your Presence in our world everywhere.
In your name and Spirit,
  help me to reach out hands of help and hope to others.
This is the day you have made,
  this day and tomorrow and tomorrow.
Let me rejoice and be glad in them all. *Amen.*

FOR PASSION SUNDAY

O Lord, I ask for faith enough to accept the love
    which has been revealed to me in him.
Keep me from twitching and wriggling away
    from the Cross of Jesus.
Keep me from banking it with flowers
    and hiding it behind fine words.
For if it is to mean anything real,
   it must stand in the deep places of my heart.
It must become a vantage point from which to interpret life.
It must mean that I too will enter into the pain of life
    and bear some measure of participation
      in the agony of being.
It must mean I cannot hold aloof
    from a world of suffering and hatred and division.
It must mean that I shall be willing to enter into life
    with all of its sorrow and its joy.
Help me to find its exact meaning for myself—
    at home,
      in the community,
        in personal relations of all kinds.
Help me, for the meaning of the Cross is not easy to find.
Somehow I know it is a spirit of life and a way of being
    that only comes as I keep as close as possible to you.

I know that our world is desperately in need
    of new ways of understanding.
We human beings still follow
   the ancient paths of war and slaughter,
    of greed and destruction.
Help us to seek new ways—
    ways of cooperation and mutual respect,
    ways of human dignity and responsible relationships.
Help us in our national and international life.
Help us in the church and in our communities.

I confess that I am hard to help
   for I get my back up when things go differently
    from the way in which I think they ought to go.

But I am grateful that you do not quit.
I am grateful for your amazing patience
  and for that flint-hard love that never gives in.
I am grateful.
Let me be grateful enough to respond with some small measure
  of the same kind of love in my relationships.
Give me more of your spirit. *Amen.*

ON PALM SUNDAY

O God of life and of being,
   I know how it must have been for those people long ago
      who rejoiced when Jesus came to their city
         and cried, "Hosanna!"
I know how their hearts swelled with good will
   and how happily they threw their hats in the air.
I know, too, when I look within,
   how the good will faded,
      and the rancorous ill will grew into the cry,
        "Crucify him!"
For I, too, am capable of swinging from praise to denial,
      from singing to cursing.
I am not always steady and sure in what I want,
   in my loves and loyalties.

I can rejoice when it is time for rejoicing,
   sing when it is time for singing,
      and praise when it is time for praising.
And I can be grateful that when I forget you
      and follow less worthy inclinations,
   you do not forget me.
O Lord, I wish you did not have to haul me back so often
      from my erring ways.
But I am grateful that you do,
   and that your love is as persistent as it is.
Give me more of the flavor of your kind of love in my life,
   so that I can be more open to others,
      more creative and responsive to the beauty and splendor
        that life can afford.
Since you refuse to give up on me,
   help me to refuse to give up on myself.

As I move toward the celebration of the great, glad news of Easter,
   lift up my heart, my whole life. *Amen.*

FOR EASTER SUNDAY

Christ is risen!
Thanks be to you, O God,
  who has raised him from the dead,
  and who, with him, has raised me from the darkness into light,
    from trembling into hope,
    from forlornness and forsakenness
      into acceptance and restoration.
I am grateful, O God.
Sometimes I forget,
  and live as though the tomb were sealed
    and the stone in place.
But on this day I remember
  and am ashamed that I live such an unresurrected life
    so much of the time.

Help me in remembering to feel the touch of resurrection within,
  to hear the voices of angels and the wild whispers of faith,
    that because he lives I shall live also.
I shall live with a new shining
  upon the dark places of hurt and heartache.
I shall live with a new vision of what it means
  to see daily existence glimmering
    in the light of an eternal purpose.
I shall live, not cringing in fear and abject in sorrow,
  but renewed in hope and assurance.

I confess how often I am ensnared
  by the despair of this ofttimes desperate world.
I read of wars and of hatreds among people,
    of the death visited upon human spirits
      by the frustrations and angers
    of a world of conflict and injustice.
I feel the tensions of misunderstanding and estrangement.
I touch broken things in my own life,
    touch them gingerly for the hurt remains,
  and the bitterness lurks close to the surface.
I cannot be put off with easy answers to hard questions.
I resent pretense and suspect piety.

My heart lies abed from sheer inertia,
   and my spirits remain indoors with the shades drawn.
I am afraid to venture out into life and love.
Then the cry is raised:

   "Christ is Risen!

   He is risen from the dead."

And suddenly I feel the thrill and the exhilaration
   of this Eastertime.

So I ask this day for a new beginning for myself.
 I admit I have asked it before.
   and then slid rapidly back into the old unresurrected ways.
But I ask it again:
O Lord, make this a day of resurrection for me,
   a day of new beginnings,
   a day of new commitment.
Raise my spirit from its tomb of selfishness and greed,
      from its burial cloths of pride and arrogance.
Free me into the resurrection life our Lord has promised.

Let me hear the thunder and the whisper,
   the trumpet and the far-off music
      of the life yet to be in him.
Thanks be to you, O God,
      through the Risen Christ. *Amen.*